BIOGRAPHIES OF OUR *Paternal* FAMILY HISTORY

"Honor your own stories and tell
them too…they are what binds families
and makes each of us who we are."

—MADELEINE L'ENGLE

Marc D. Thompson

FRONT COVER PHOTOGRAPHS

TOP LEFT: Myrtle Batdorf   MIDDLE: Irvin Duncan
BOTTOM LEFT: Mamie Anderson   BOTTOM RIGHT: Harper Thompson

Family histories require constant revision.
Please contact the author with any corrections or additions at
info@marcdthompson.net.

Published by:

VirtuFit Press
Delray Beach, FL
www.marcdthompson.net
info@marcdthompson.net

ISBN: 978-0-99080-743-8

Interior and cover design: Gary A. Rosenberg • www.thebookcouple.com

Printed in the United States of America

This volume includes the following families:

Thompson, Russell, Penman, Stoddart, Goodman, Brown, Carl, Hensel, Guise, Workman, Romberger, Updegrove, Reisch, Culp, Schneck, Batdorf, Steiner, Welker, Messerschmidt, Peters, DeHart, Swartz, Koval, Wert, Faber, Shoop, Wertz, Row, Rudy, Frantz, Gieseman, Duncan, Westphals, Kelling, Koppelmann, McCloud, Searfoss, Kankle, Layman, Klein, Raymond, Roush, Overlander, Warner, Gipe, Drust, Anderson, Arnold, Bordner, Emerich, Gaugler, Kelly, Shaffer, Keefer, Arnold(2), Bucher, Mantz, Livezly, Culin, Kent, Roberts, et al., from Southcentral England, Southeast Scotland, Ireland, East Finland, Central Sweden, South & Northeast Germany, and Northcentral Switzerland emigrated to Pennsylvania, New York, Virginia, and Louisiana.

OTHER BOOKS BY MARC D. THOMPSON

*This volume is dedicated to all our family and friends,
who selflessly donated information, time, effort, research,
and love to make this compilation possible.*

Acknowledgments

Thanks to my parents, to my sisters, and my children for the knowledge and support. Thanks to my history teachers through school and college. Thanks to Ray from Pennsylvania State Library for his early tutelage. Thanks to my hundreds of cousins, near and far, who have donated their time as well as their long-toiled family histories. Thanks to every clerk, registrar, cemetery manager, LDS employee, ancestry.com staff, and others who researched in places I couldn't visit. Thanks to the amazing literary talents of Tom Sullivan, Jack Smiles, Alicia Craig, Mason Smith, and Talea Jurrens as well as the incomparable editing and layout skills of Carol and Gary Rosenberg. This book is truly the love of thousands.

Contents

Foreword

by Heather Thompson-Green

When I was asked to write the foreword for this book, I was honored, not only because I feel it is an important part of this book, but because it is also my family history, and that makes me extremely proud to be a part of something so exciting. Marc is a dedicated author, with this Narrative being the updated completion and compilation of the earlier volume. His interest in well-being is also evident to those who know him, and proven in his research.

Family history, or genealogy, is not "just" history. It is where you came from, who you are, and what you pass on to those who follow. What we learn about ourselves can easily be traced back to where we came from, and understanding that is knowledge we take with us.

As you read this Compendium, it will inspire you to dig into your own genealogy and pass along interesting facts about the amazing family you come from. Perhaps you will find a glimmer of a royal connection that will excite you, and lead you to investigate your history a little further. Tracing your father's, grandfather's, or great-grandfather's footsteps is not only educational and necessary, but fun as well.

Marc has done the hard part, so I hope you enjoy his work and dedication to our family lineage. Be the ambassador for your family as well, and enjoy the education of finding where your family began.

Introduction

As Malcolm Gladwell says, "Who we are cannot be separated from where we're from." Genealogy is a duty. The day we were born or the day we bore children ourselves, we gained a responsibility of passing along our history. We are responsible for the knowledge of our parents and of our grandparents and all the wisdom that comes with this knowledge. Our duty, therefore, includes our children's heritage—including the names and faces of their forefathers and mothers, the medical history and genetic backgrounds of their blood lines, the princes and the paupers, the photographs and historical areas and properties, the tragedies and the joys.

If I were given the opportunity to live in any era, I would most certainly pick the 1870s. The time was simple and the people were honest. Folks worked hard and took pride in their families, their homes and their reputations. When I look into the eyes of our ancestors from that time period, I feel a link; I would have fit nicely in their time.

Genealogy was created in order for people to know the history of their lineage, to discover their origins, and to prove blood-lines and royalty. This volume was compiled in response to our deep desire to understand and discover their past. It shall stand as part of the legacy of their ancestry. Our ancestors had remembrances. They had goals, glories, and personalities. The Irish kings would pass down their regal history orally. They would recite a list of names—their kin—noting outstanding events associated with the forbearers. The ancient Scottish bards similarly memorized their royal families, reciting the pedigrees of the Old Scot's Kings regardless of the complexity.

Our 35-year journey of knowledge has led to a plethora of information. We have learned much. We have discovered our roots—good, bad, and ugly. It has molded us. It has given us information on our health and ways to stay fit and healthy. It has given us photographs, the opportunity to see ourselves in generations gone by, noting how our features and personalities have evolved. It has helped with our jobs, our relationships, our lives. Our ancestors are a mirror of ourselves that can aide in our survival and understanding. Ancestry is wisdom.

Our journey has led to the numerous volumes of the Thompson Family History (TFH), of which this follows and updates the previous volumes. In most cases, the Anglicized first and middle names were used throughout the Narrative. For example, Johann Heinrich is John Henry and Orsala Francesca is Ursula Frances. The most commonly found surname was used, whether Anglicized or not. The majority of the collateral information was derived from the U.S. Census records and cousins' data.

Additionally, place names were documented as precisely as possible, using the name of the place as it was at that time in history. For example, parts of Germany were once Prussia, parts of Lebanon County, Pennsylvania were once Lancaster County, Pennsylvania. However in some cases, the common name was used. Before Pennsylvania's statehood, although it was the Swedish Colony and later the Province of Pennsylvania, simply Pennsylvania was used. This holds true to cities, provinces and countries as well. Lastly, to preserve privacy, all information on living persons has been removed or privatized.

Many genealogies tend to trace a descendant line or the paternal line (single ascendancy). Our purpose was to trace all ancestors with equal perseverance back in time. This is a monumental—if not near impossible—task. We have compiled a pedigree, beginning with our children and using an ahnentafel format. The emphasis at present is on generations 1 through 10, although we have completed research as far back as generation 21. Additional collateral ancestors have begun to be added as of 2015.

The mission of our genealogy books is four-fold. First, to amass photographs—as a face can tell a thousand tales—as so much can be learned from them. The second goal is to document the medical background of our ancestors, so our children can lead a healthier life. The third goal is to continue to extend the lineage in order to link to as many relatives as possible. Our ancestors are not mere names or dates—they have tales to tell, journeys to document, lives to discover. They have accomplishments and setbacks, which in turn help us with ours. Our final goal leads us to the building of narratives from this amassed information, producing a readable experience of our ancestors and their lives. As we mentioned "Who we are cannot be separated from where we're from," this book therefore allows us to know precisely where we're from.

As this century moves along, more and more information becomes digitally or electronically disposable. If we do not save this information, it may be lost forever. The Thompson Family History is a guide for future generations who may use this information for their own goals, whatever they may be. We have given our children a foundation. Take it, improve it, embrace it.

What's In a Name?

Other children, as with all life, represent the beginning of all things. They are bore and they begin their life-long experiences. Here they are the beginning of our book, back from which we narrate to bring their ancestors to life. Our children, nephews and nieces were all born from 1980–2010. Here are some of the meanings behind our children's names.

Adam: This is the Hebrew word for "man." It could be ultimately derived from Hebrew אדם (Adam) meaning "to be red," referring to the ruddy color of human skin, or from Akkadian adamu meaning "to make." According to Genesis in the Old Testament, Adam was created from the earth by God. There is a word play on Hebrew אֲדָמָה (adamah) "earth." He and Eve were supposedly the first humans, living happily in the Garden of Eden until Adam ate a forbidden fruit given to him by Eve. As an English Christian name, Adam has been common since the Middle Ages, and it received a boost after the Protestant Reformation. A famous bearer was Scottish economist Adam Smith (1723–1790).

Andrew: English form of the Greek name Ανδρεας (Andreas), which was derived from ανδρειος (andreios) "manly, masculine," a derivative of ανηρ (aner) "man." In the New Testament the apostle Andrew, the first disciple to join Jesus, is the brother of Simon Peter. According to tradition, he later preached in the Black Sea region, with some legends saying he was crucified on an X-shaped cross. Andrew, being a Greek name, was probably only a nickname or a translation of his real Hebrew name, which is not known. This name has been common throughout the Christian world, and it became very popular in the Middle Ages.

Saint Andrew is regarded as the patron of Scotland, Russia, Greece and Romania. The name has been borne by three kings of Hungary, American president Andrew Jackson and, more recently, English composer Andrew Lloyd Webber.

Ashley: From an English surname which was originally derived from place names meaning "ash tree clearing," from Old English *æsc* and *Leah*. Until the 1960s it was more commonly given to boys in the United States, but it is now most often used on girls.

Connor: Anglicized form of the Gaelic name *Conchobhar* which means "dog lover" or "wolf lover." It has been in use in Ireland for centuries and was the name of several Irish kings. It was also borne by the legendary Ulster King *Conchobar mac Nessa,* known for his tragic desire for Deirdre.

Marie: French and Czech form of Maria. A notable bearer of this name was Marie Antoinette, a queen of France, and Marie Curie, a physicist and chemist who studied radioactivity with her husband Pierre. Latin form of Greek Μαρια, from Hebrew מִרְיָם (Mary). Maria is the usual form of the name in many European languages, as well as a secondary form in other languages such as English. In some countries, for example Germany, Poland and Italy, Maria is occasionally used as a masculine middle name. This was the name of two ruling queens of Portugal. It was also borne by the Habsburg queen Maria Theresa, whose inheritance of the domains of her father, the Holy Roman Emperor Charles VI, began the War of the Austrian Succession. The meaning is not known for certain, but there are several theories including "sea of bitterness," "rebelliousness," and "wished for child." However it was most likely originally an Egyptian name, perhaps derived in part from my "beloved" or my "love."

Renae: French form of Renatus. A famous bearer was the French mathematician and rationalist philosopher René Descartes. Late Latin name meaning "born again."

Roman: From the Late Latin name Romanus which meant "Roman."

Sophia: Means "wisdom" in Greek. This was the name of an early, probably mythical, saint who died of grief after her three daughters were martyred.

Legends about her probably arose as a result of a medieval misunderstanding of the phrase Hagia Sophia "Holy Wisdom," which was the name of a large basilica in Constantinople. This name was common among continental European royalty during the Middle Ages, and it was popularized in Britain by the German House of Hanover when they inherited the British throne in the 18th century. It was the name of characters in the novels *Tom Jones* by Henry Fielding and *The Vicar of Wakefield* by Oliver Goldsmith.

※

Through the research of the TFH, we have discovered that we are related to some famous and infamous folks, and even found that there are some areas of the world named for our distant families. We are direct-line descendants of William Duke of Jülich-Cleves-Berg and Maria of Austria, Duchess of Jülich-Cleves-Berg, Countess Clothilde de Valois de Reni and Jacques de Sellaire, Von Zeller of Castle Zellerstein of Zurich, John Thomson of Haddington, Johann La Hentzelle of Lorraine, General John Benfield of Normandy, Henri Banage de Beauval of Rouen, Alexander Thompson of Schuylkill, the Guerne family of Eschert, the Bager family of Wiesbaden, the Emmerich family of Delkenheim, the Batdorf family of Darmstadt, the Gaukel family of Miltenberg and the Lotz family of the Palatinate.

We are direct-line descendants of soldiers who sacrificed for our freedom: Civil War servicemen Andrew G. Hensel and Daniel Updegrove, and possibly Elijah Anderson and Thomas E. Batdorf. War of 1812 servicemen Adam Frantz, Andrew W. Hensel and Joseph Workman, and possible William Row and John Gipe. Revolutionary War servicemen Andrew Messerschmidt, Andrew Miller, Frank Row, Henry Bucher, Jacob Lehman, Jacob Livezey, Jacob Philip Bordner, Jacob Rudy, John Adam Guise, John Balthaser Romberger, John Casper Hensel, John Conrad Bucher, John Daniel Angst, John Faber, John George Herrold, John George Schupp, John Henry Reiman, John Jacob Loyman John Miller, John Peter Braun (British), John Peter Shaffer, Jonas Rudy, Michael Garman, Michael Leyman, Nicholas Mantz, Peter Keefer, Valentine Welker, and William Anderson.

Our ancestors' names have been immortalized at these locations: the Bager Homestead, Abbottstown, Pennsylvania; the Chris Miller Homestead, North

Lebanon Township, Pennsylvania; the Benfield Homestead, Berks Co., Pennsylvania; the Livesey Homestead, Philadelphia, Pennsylvania; the Wirth Homestead, Dauphin Co., Pennsylvania; the Keefer Homestead in Berks, Pennsylvania; the Morton Homestead in Chester, Pennsylvania; the Herrold Homestead in Northumberland, Pennsylvania; and the Jacob Lehman Homestead in Hanover, Pennsylvania. Additionally, these place names were named after our forebearers: Bordnersville, Kelly Crossroads, Livesey Street, Herrold's Island, Keefer's Station, Deibler's Gap, Deibler's Dam, and Shoemakertown, all in Pennsylvania.

Our children's maternal lines include WWII servicemen Ed Mazo, Percy Forsythe and Robert Forsythe; WWI serviceman Raymond Barbush; and Civil War servicemen Cyrus Shannon, Jacob Wittle, John Shover, John Minnick, and Sebastian Shover. We are collateral descendants of Presidents Dwight D. Eisenhower and William McKinley; Pennsylvania politicians Samuel Pennypacker, John Morton, and Jonas Row; Civil War Brigadier General Galushia Pennypacker; entertainers Marlon Brando, Les Brown, and Ray W. Brown; religious leaders Conrad Weiser and Michael Enderline; and famed Melba Dodge, Jesse Runkle, Enrico Caruso, and Galla Curci. Lastly, Taylor Wittel lists relations to James Madison, Zachary Taylor, Jefferson Davis, and Gene Autry.

At the moment, our paternal line breaks down to about 11/16 German, 2/16 Scottish, 1/16 French, 1/16 Swiss, 1/32 English, and 1/32 Dutch-Bohemian. Our maternal line breaks down to about 10/16 German, 4/16 English, 1/16 French, 1/32 Swiss and 1/32 Scandanavian. The approximate percentages of relatives birthplaces are: 45% born in Pennsylvania, 17% Germany, 14% Scotland, 9% Italy, 4% Georgia, 4% South Carolina, 4% Ireland, 2% New York, and 1% Virginia, Florida, Switzerland, England, Bohemia, France, Sweden, Finland, and the West Indies.

This Thompson Family History volume will serve to honor us with the researched and documented information of our background. Our ancestry was derived from this data, which includes numbers. Here are some interesting numerical facts.

3 Ancestors who died at sea: N. Benesch, G. Reith & G. Shoemaker

3 Ancestors named Ashley or Renae

5 Number of birth states

8 Ancestors named Gerald or Gilbert

8 Most different lines with same surname: Miller, Mueller, etc.

10 Generations, FTM lines only (numerous)

11 Number of birth countries

14 Youngest age having child, female: Anna Maria Hamm & Anna Barbara Knerr

17 Youngest age having child, male, John George Werner

17 Number of children, one couple, Mary Louisa Peters/ Thomas Edward Batdorf

18 Youngest age at death, female: Emma Keefer

21 Generations, FTM & additional lines (Livesay)

22 Number of children, one man, Isabelle Penman & Mary Bast/Alexander Thompson

24 Ancestors named Sophia or Marie

24 Most letters in name, male: Howard Andrew Carson Hensel

27 Most letters in name, female: Amelia Dorothy Elizabeth Bager

30 Youngest age at death, male: William Duncan

34 Ancestors named Andrew or Roman

34 Media records, collateral lines

50 Oldest age having child, female: Veronica Schmidt

50+ Most variations for single surname: Batdorf, Bodorff, Batterff, Pottorf, etc.

57 Ancestors named Connor or Adam

59.6 Average lifespan, all lines

63.2 Average lifespan, Thompson lines

68 Oldest age having child, male: Alexander Thompson

79 Media records, maternal lines

94 Oldest age at death: Sarah Faber, Anna Bleymeyer & Michael Goodman

254 Media records, Thompson lines

256 Ancestors named Shirley or Mary

405 Sources used, maternal lines

569 Direct-line ancestors, Thompson lines

846 Sources used, Thompson lines

870 Direct-line ancestors

595 Place names, maternal lines

776 Place names, Thompson lines

987 Total surnames, Thompson line

1,230 Total surnames

1410 Earliest birth, unrecorded lines, Geoffrey Livesay

1689 Earliest birth, recorded lines, John Wendel George Traut

5,750 Sources checked

5,801 Relatives, Thompson lines

8,571 Relatives

41,178 Kilobytes TFH Family Tree Maker File

This and the proceeding Thompson Family History narratives are our heritage. With this information we can be proud of ourselves and our past, and aim toward a bright future and better lives. If our duty is neglected, as each generation passes, so will our family history. We have a desire and we have a bond. We have a desire to know from whence we came. We want to know our history, our origins. We want to know what our ancestors did, how they persevered and how the spark of life made its way from Geoffrey Livesay, born 1410 in England, to our latest cousin, born just this winter 2015. We feel that bond.

CHAPTER 1

Generation One

Children travel from the heart to the heart.
—SWEDISH PROVERB

The following narrative is an outline of the family, places, times and activities of the author, Marc D. Thompson of Harrisburg, PA. The narrative is brief but gives insight into the background, history upbringing and personality of time.

This generation includes my two sisters, my 77 first cousins, and so many of the baby boomers around the country, most born in the 1960s and 1970s. History is important, exciting, educational and fun and allows our generation and our children a better understand.

For our children, this constitutes the paternal lines from myself back. The next published volume will include all the maternal lines and their narratives and lineage.

Here are some of the meanings behind our names:

Ann: French form of *Anna*. In the 13th-century it was imported to England, where it was also commonly spelled *Ann*. The name was borne by a 17th-century English queen and also by the second wife of Henry VIII, Anne Boleyn, the mother of Queen Elizabeth I. This is also the name of the heroine in *Anne of Green Gables* by Canadian author L. M. Montgomery.

Duncan: Anglicized form of the Gaelic name *Donnchadh* meaning "brown warrior," derived from Gaelic *donn* "brown" and *cath* "warrior." This was the name of two kings of Scotland, including the one who was featured in Shakespeare's play *Macbeth*. Originally German *Dunkart*, a North German nickname from Middle Low German *dunker* meaning "dark," "conceited," or "unclear."

Elaine: From an Old French form of *Helen*. It appears in Arthurian legend; in Thomas Malory's 15th-century compilation *Le Morte d'Arthur*, Elaine was the daughter of Pelleas, the lover of Lancelot, and the mother of Galahad. It was not commonly used as an English given name until after the appearance of Tennyson's Arthurian epic *Idylls of the King*.

Jill: Medieval English feminine form of *Julian*. This spelling has been in use since the 13th century, though it was not declared a distinct name from Julian until the 17th century.

Marc: Form of *Marcus*. Saint Mark was the author of the second Gospel in the New Testament. He is the patron saint of Venice, where he is supposedly buried. Though in use during the Middle Ages, Mark was not common in the English-speaking world until the 19th century, when it began to be used alongside the classical form Marcus. In the Celtic legend of Tristan and Isolde, this was the name of a king of Cornwall. It was also borne by the American author Mark Twain—real name Samuel Clemens—the author of *Tom Sawyer* and *Huckleberry Finn*. He actually took his pen name from a call used by riverboat workers on the Mississippi River to indicate a depth of two fathoms. This is also the usual English spelling of the name of the 1st-century BC Roman triumvir Marcus Antonius (Mark Antony).

Tory: Diminutive of *Victoria*. Means "victory" in Latin, being borne by the Roman goddess of victory. It is also a feminine form of *Victorius*. This name was borne by a 4th-century saint and martyr from North Africa. Though in use elsewhere in Europe, the name was very rare in the English-speaking world until the 19th century, when Queen Victoria began her long rule of Britain. She was named after her mother, who was of German royalty. Many geographic areas are named after the queen, including an Australian state and a Canadian city.

PART ONE: **The First 30 Years, 1964–1993**

Marc Duncan Thompson's father was from Lykens, Pennsylvania and his mother was from Hummel's Wharf, Pennsylvania. His father was the son of Myrtle Batdorf of Big Run, Pennsylvania and Harper Thompson of Sheridan, Pennsylvania and his mother was the daughter of Mamie Anderson of Jackson, Pennsylvania and Irvin Duncan of Sunbury, Pennsylvania.

Marc spent quality time with both set of grandparents and he remembers two of his great-grandparents, Beulah Batdorf and Gussie Mae Hensel. Marc is the youngest of three children, having two sisters, one who is married to Mr. Shannon and one who is married to Mr. Nee.

As a youth, Marc recalls how his sisters loved to collect and play 45 rpm records. As children, his mother gave them numerous responsibilities. She taught them to wash their clothes, cook and "red up" their rooms. His mother did their ironing, one chore he found and still deems useless. His mother also used to prepare cheese sandwiches by "ironing" then while wrapped in aluminum foil. Although his mother did sew, most of his clothes were purchased. She would buy him Sears Toughskin jeans because he always wore out the knees playing. Marc has always enjoyed wearing simple clothes, jeans, t-shirt and sneakers. That is still his garb of choice.

Marc's family occasionally drove to see his mother's parents, Mamie and Irvin, in Hummel's Wharf, Pennsylvania. His mother wanted to use their first names instead of grandpa or grandpa. The family however more often visited his father's parents, Myrtle and Harper, as they lived close by on Lexington Street in Harrisburg. Marc like Harper however he disliked going there when Aunt Gerry was there because she would come rushing to him and squeeze his cheeks. As a youngster, they also visited his mother's sister's family, in Shiremanstown, Pennsylvania and his mother's brother family in Mt. Gretna. Marc's family did not entertain often but they did go to many family gatherings.

He was on honor roll at school and enjoyed sports, biking and reading. He also wore his hair long throughout middle and high school. He recalls the funerals of Gussie, Irvin, Mamie and Harper. He was at college when his Myrtle passed and unfortunately was unable to attend her funeral.

As an infant, Marc lived in a house on 6th Street in Harrisburg, Pennsylvania. When he was one, the family moved to a country house, on Peter's Mountain

Road in Matamoras, Pennsylvania. They moved again when he was eight, from Matamoras to a wonderful suburban home in Rutherford Heights, PA at 280 South 67th Street, Harrisburg, PA. The isolation of the rural house was unbearable and the suburban house was a welcomed gift. He lived in Rutherford Heights until he attended college.

The Matamoras abode was a small gray faux-stone two-bedroom house. The house included a small living room and kitchen. His parents used the den on the first floor as a bedroom and the second floor had two very small bedrooms, one room for his sisters and one for me. There was a basement where the kids occasionally played.

Marc used to ride his bike around the front lawn and driveway, setting up pretend streets and street signs. Once he injured his head trying to ride his tricycle down the declined driveway backwards. The backyard was $3/4$ of an acre and the kids often played kick the can, hide and seek, and softball.

Along the south side were a row of pine trees, one for each Christmas they had in Matamoras. The North side of the lawn had a row of weeping willow trees on which he used to play Tarzan. There was a large white brick fireplace in the backyard and would occasionally have cookouts. A lazy creek ran through the backyard. One day grandpa Irvin, while trying to escape the family dog, fell into the creek.

Marc enjoyed Rutherford most of all. It was a split level red brick home with three bedrooms and $1^1/2$ baths, a large rec room and an even larger basement. His bedroom was in at least five different rooms during his time there. There was a sun room off the kitchen and a patio and fenced backyard. He used to perform magic and puppet shows in the basement. The second bathroom in the cellar became a graffiti room where everyone who visited left a message on the walls. He used to slide down the laundry chute that went from the top floor bathroom to the laundry room. The home was situated right at the circle in the neighborhood. This was a great place for all the neighborhood kids to meet up.

In Matamoras, the family ate in the kitchen. His mother rang a dinner bell to alert the kids it was time to eat. He would sneak baked potato skins to his sisters because he didn't like them. They would pick cherries and berries and often would husk corn, some of which they grew themselves. His mother often canned goods and stored them in the basement. He recalls milk pies and mashed turnips. One November a severe snow storm knocked out the electricity and they ate scrambled eggs cooked on a potbelly stove for Thanksgiving. They had well water.

In Rutherford, they ate in the dining room. All three siblings prepared one dinner per week. His favorite food to prepare was mashed potatoes. They cooked on an electric stove and had a microwave oven as early as 1978 that his mother won in a contest.

Because his parents divorced and both his sister were older, it shortly became just his mother and he. The home was heated by oil which was delivered regularly and they had city water. His mother used to light many candles. They had a fireplace that lured him to bed many nights.

In Matamoras, he first remembers a small white dog named Ardy and a large brown dog, aptly named Sandy. Ardy was an energetic pup who ran around the house. Sandy lived outside in his dog house in the backyard. Sandy was the dog that chased Irvin into the creek. His one sister had a white cat named Snowflakes but became known simply as Kitty. She definitely had nine lives, including, among other tragedies, being hit by a car and being trapped in a burning barn.

His father was a hunter and hence had a hunting beagle named Stormy. Stormy was born the same time as he and lived a long life. She was a great pet and hunter. Her name was apropos as she was not friendly. Marc is an adamant anti-hunter. They used to go deer sighting in the countryside of Matamoras, something Marc enjoyed.

Marc was given a gray tiger cat, who unfortunately ran away at the drive-in theatres. A short lived pet parenthood. In Rutherford, his mother bought his sister a white Shepherd-Husky mix. Her name was Queenie and she soon learned to jump over the backyard fence and roam the neighborhood. She was fun to play with and was big enough to ride like a horse. After his eldest sister left the house, Queenie was cared by the middle sister and then Marc. When Marc went to college, Queenie given to a friend's father. She became a seeing-eye dog for him as he aged, helping him get around his farm. He had a number of pet goldfish and a rabbit, but he has always thought pet ownership needs to be taken more seriously and could be quite restrictive for most animals. He didn't want a pet if he didn't have the means to give them a full and happy life.

His father was a master electrician, working that trade his entire life. His mother was a homemaker and was later employed in many capacities, worked predominantly at the CIA in Washington DC. Marc's first job was delivering the

Guide newspaper throughout Rutherford Heights. He started at age thirteen and earned five cents per paper delivered. He worked at Mitgang's Coin and Stamp Store on Clearfield Street doing inventory where he was paid in stamps. He also worked in Hanover Shoes at the Harrisburg East Mall during high school. These were all part-time jobs, and he secured his first full-time job at Hersheypark in High School and worked there throughout high school and college. While at college, He worked as a full time evening Pizzeria manager. After college graduation, he began his career as a Personal Trainer and Genealogist.

His father occasionally planted a garden, something Marc currently follows. In Matamoras, they grew strawberries and had a vegetable garden. In Rutherford, they had a small vegetable garden in the backyard. They didn't raise any livestock, but his father once bought ducklings that he raised to adulthood and then used for duck soup!

His father also hunted regularly and brought home various animals. Marc knew at an early age that hunting was unchallenging, so decided to find challenges elsewhere. The regular meals were meat and potatoes. The family used to make home-made ice cream in the basement in Matamoras. Marc recognized at a young age to eat healthy and changed the way he ate.

He enjoyed astronomy at an early age and would buy any astronomical item he could find. He also enjoyed paleontology and would regularly search for fossils. He enjoyed instructing and teaching and used to have magic shows, card shows, etc. for his family and neighbors. He enjoyed music most of all, listening to radios and buying albums when he had jobs to earn money.

Marc admired his grandfather Harper, who was always calm and thoughtful, kind and gentle. Also being tall, Marc looked up to him literally and figuratively. Marc's mother taught him patience, perseverance and frugality. His father taught him planning, discipline and teaching. Marc was influenced by his Biology teacher, Mr. Killinger, his Uncle Ray who helped him apply to college and Bob Griese, Miami Dolphins quarterback, who was a great calm sport tactician and planner. Siri Neal was his yoga teacher and Sarah Johnson was his swim coach. Both have influenced him positively. He learned business sense from Keith Cooper, Vice-president of White Shield, Inc. Marc has been fortunate to have many ethical righteous independent people in his life.

Marc was in the Cub Scouts and on the Y swim team. As a youngster, his hobbies included sports, astronomy, stamp collecting, magic, bike riding, music and reading. As a teen he also enjoyed all sports, fitness, photography, genealogy, games, writing, poetry and hiking. He always enjoyed teaching and assembling items. He loved movies and music. He once saw Star Wars over twenty times at the theatres.

During the summers he would work, do sports, ride bike, read and swim. He went to Wildwood regularly throughout middle and high school. He learned to play drums and horseback ride. He recalls taking many walks and hikes. They walked from the Matamoras house to a Swimming Hole called Hunky Dam. He also walked from Tower City to Rutherford with his father.

His best friends in Matamoras were his neighbors Bradley Shaffer and Bart. Once he started Elementary School he befriended Troy Gingrich and Bernie Weiss. In Rutherford, he enjoyed sports and played football at Jeff Heffner's house, waffle ball at Jeff Maxwell's house and Hockey at the School playground. He became friends with Jeff Maxwell and Mike Herbein. In Middle and High School he was part of a group of five friends, including Jeff, Mike, Mike Wilbert and Dan Leonard. Jeff and he attended college together and he became friends with Dave Gauntt, Barrett Windish, Jim Vetter, Kerr Nee, Mike Thompson, Chris Honer and Scott Quinerly.

The first car he remembers the family owning was a tan Pontiac, possible a Lemans, and later a green Pontiac Tempest. His mother taught him to drive by driving the Tempest down local alleys. His father took him to Dauphin County Vo-Tech parking lot to prepare for his driver's license and he first drove on Locust Lane. His first car was the hand-me-down Tempest that went from his father to his sister to him. He also owned a Nissan pickup, Oldsmobile wagon, Buick Regal and Ford Taurus.

His first train ride was to Sunbury to see his mother's parents and his first plane trip was to Denver to see his sister. He has taken many boat rides. In Matamoras, there very few businesses near us. They had to travel over 25 miles over Peter's Mountain to find a mini-market. There was a gas station and a drive-in theatre near us. For anything else, they had to travel into Harrisburg, nearly an hour away. He liked going to People's Drug store to look at the toys and get a vanilla milk shake. He also enjoyed Zimmerman's Grocery, a natural health food store that smelled so deliciously of roasted nuts.

In Rutherford, he could walk or bike to nearly anywhere. He liked going to the Harrisburg East Mall, to play sports, the Star skate arena, Hersheypark, etc.

They never visited any large cities as a family and he recalls the only two family vacations were to Virginia and Maine.

He attended Halifax Elementary School from first through third grade; He was picked up by a school bus. He completed elementary school at Rutherford, where he walked to school and then he went to Lawnton for sixth grade, Central Dauphin Middle and Central Dauphin High Schools. The TMI alert occurred when he was in Mr. Bonner's ninth grade classroom.

He usually packed a lunch until high school and he enjoyed science, writing, poetry, math, spelling bees and SRA's. He took college prep classes, played many intramurals and was on the band as a drummer. He attended Moravian College and earned a Bachelor's degree in pre-Med and Biology. He was active in Biology, Art Computer Science clubs as well as the WRMC radio station. He worked as a DJ and also played intramurals each year in softball, volleyball and ultimate Frisbee. Marc was blessed with his first child Ashley.

PART TWO: **The Second 30 Years, 1994–2023**

Marc was doubled blessed in the late 90's with children Andrew and Connor. Two amazing sons to carry on the family name. Fortunately during this time he divorced and eventually found his soulmate, Melvalean Curry. Melvalean and he married in September, 2001. Mel was born in Philadelphia, PA and is the daughter of Dolores Ann Curry & Eddie Mazo from Savannah, GA. Their daughter Sophia was born in 2004.

Marc and Mel lived in Philadelphia, PA and moved to Delray Beach, Florida in 2003. They spent a brief time in Narberth and Haverford, Pennsylvania and in Boynton Beach and Boca Raton, Florida. They purchased a house in Delray in December 2007.

Mel had previous children, Tiffany and Tyler. Mel worked as a calligrapher and was beginning her career in real estate. Tragically, Mel passed away in May 2008 in an unexpected accident. She was a wonderful woman and wife, a beautiful soul and dedicated mother. Her wondrous energy live son in us today. She will never be forgotten.

Marc continued his self-employment as a personal trainer adding professional fitness consultant and professional genealogist. He published numerous genealogy books, poems and exhibited photographs. He published four fitness book and one compilation of poetry. He built his first website www.VirtuFit.ner and has embarked on solidifying his virtual training career, now toting 8 websites including www.marcdthompson.net.

Sophia won three beauty pageants at an early age and did modeling in Miami. She has an agent in Miami and is frequently called for go-sees and modeling shoots. Sophia is also taking Gymnastics and modeling. Sophia is smart, beautiful and intuitive. She enjoys dance, music, art and gymnastics.

Ashley finished High School, receiving good grades. She wants to go to college and become a teacher. She recently moved back to Hershey. Andrew is an amazing pianist and great swimmer. He is a wise boy and is very creative. Connor is carefree, confident and tough. He is excelled in school and has fun. Tiffany is working in Philadelphia and moving to a new apartment. Tyler is doing in Coatesville, PA. He is very athletic and fun.

Marc continues to eat healthy and eat almost anything. He loves to try new restaurants and the area has many to offer. He travels often and own a Ford

Expedition and a Ford Flex. He has vacationed to Canada, Mexico, Dominican Republic, Puerto Rico, Costa Rica, Bahamas, Jamaica, Washington, Colorado, Oregon, DC, Alaska, Illinois, and all the states on Eastern seaboard. He has continued his education taking numerous fitness and genealogy programs. He enjoys movies, music and people. He continues his wellness knowledge, bringing health to clients and writing books. He is excited to see what his children become.

Coming in 2023!

PART THREE: **The Third 30 Years**

CHAPTER 2

※

Generation Two

Generations pass like leaves fall from our family tree.
Each season new life blossoms and grows benefiting from
the strength and experience of those who went before.
—HEIDI SWAPP

Our parents are including in the second generation, comprising those born in from about 1930 to 1950. Those living are not included in this book, so we move on to the third generation, which would be our grandparents.

Here are some of the meanings behind our parent's names:

Gerald: From a Germanic name meaning "rule of the spear," from the elements *ger* "spear" and *wald* "rule." The Normans brought this name to Britain. Though it died out in England during the Middle Ages, it remained common in Ireland. It was revived in the English-speaking world in 19th century.

Gilbert: Means "bright pledge," derived from the Germanic elements *gisil* "pledge, hostage" and *beraht* "bright." The Normans introduced this name to England, where it was common during the Middle Ages. It was borne by a 12th-century British saint, the founder of the religious order known as the Gilbertines.

Mary: Usual English form of *Maria,* the Latin form of the New Testament Greek names *Μαριαμ* and *Μαρια,* which were from Hebrew מִרְיָם (Miryam), a name borne by the sister of Moses in the Old Testament. The meaning is not known for certain, but there are several theories including "sea of bitterness," "rebelliousness," and "wished-for child." However it was most likely originally an Egyptian name, perhaps derived in part from "my beloved" or "my love." This is the name of several New Testament characters, most importantly Mary, the virgin mother of Jesus, and Mary Magdalene. Due to the Virgin Mary this name has been very popular in the Christian world, though at certain times and in some cultures it has been considered too holy for everyday use. In England it has been used since the 12th century, and it has been among the most common feminine names since the 16th century. The Latinized form *Maria* is also used in English as well as in several other languages. This name has been borne by two queens of England, as well as a Queen of Scotland—Mary Queen of Scots. Another notable bearer was Mary Shelley, the author of *Frankenstein.* A famous fictional character by this name is Mary Poppins, from the children's books by P. L. Travers.

Shirley: From a surname which was originally derived from a place name meaning "bright clearing" in Old English. This is the name of the main character in Charlotte Bronte's semi-autobiographical novel *Shirley.* The child actress Shirley Temple helped to popularize this name.

CURRENT EVENTS FOR OUR PARENTS

To place ourselves in our parent's generations, one must understand the occurrences of the time just preceding their births. Here is a brief summary of Pennsylavnia's happening from 1910 to 1930, after which most of our parents were born.

1910s

Pennsylvania Railroad began service to New York City. Rayon was 1st commercially produced by Marcus Hook in Pennsylvania. In Philadelphia John Wanamaker's The Grand Depot department store was replaced by a 250-foot tall, 12-story edifice known as Wanamaker's. Bellevue Park, first planned neighborhood in central PA, was built. The Philadelphia Athletics, forerunners of the Oakland A's, won the World Series, beating the New York Giants of the National League, today's SF Giants. Rotary Club, First service club in Harrisburg, opened. The football team of PA's Carlisle Indian School, with running back Jim Thorpe, defeated the Army team, with Dwight D. Eisenhower as linebacker, 27-6. Engraver George T. Morgan is believed to have produced 5 Liberty Head V nickels at the Philadelphia Mint with a 1913 stamped date. Leopold Stokowski was hired as the music director of the Philadelphia Orchestra. Harrisburg Riverwalk construction begun. Perry Como, singer, was born in Canonsburg. The first drive-in automobile service station, built by Gulf Refining Co., opened in Pittsburgh. In Pennsylvania a fire at the Red Ash colliery ignited a coal mine. As of 2009 it was still burning and was the oldest of 36 ongoing mine fires. The transit company reorganized as "Harrisburg Railways." Harrisburg City Beautiful continues, raises money with bonds and City library opened. Geisinger Health Systems was founded in PA. Great Migration brings many black workers to Harrisburg's steel mills. The Mercer Museum in Doylestown was completed by Henry Chapman Mercer, archeologist and collector. Bethlehem Steel takes over Pennsylvania Steel Company in Steelton. A munitions factory explosion at Eddystone, killing 133 workers. Bernstein, artist, helped found the Philadelphia Ten, a female art group. John G. Johnson, Philadelphia lawyer, died and left his home a collection of Renaissance art to the city. Outbreak of Spanish Influenza. A TNT explosion in chemical factory in Oakdale, killed 200. A race riot in Chester left three blacks and two whites dead. Milton Hershey endowed the Milton Hershey School with $60 million in stock. The influenza epidemic killed 11,000 people in Philadelphia. Penn-Harris Hotel constructed in Harrisburg. African-American YMCA branch established.

1920s

The first radio broadcast of presidential elections in the United States were made by radio. Westinghouse had built radio station KDKA on its factory roof in Pittsburgh and was among the first to broadcast returns from the Harding-Cox presidential election. 8MK, the first US station owned by a newspaper (the Detroit News), also broadcast the election returns. The 1st Thanksgiving Parade was held in Philadelphia. The last trolleys were acquired. Electricity begins to become available for most households. Religious services were first broadcast on radio. Police in Sunbury issued an edict requiring women to wear skirts at least 4 inches below the knee. The first radio broadcast of a baseball game took place in Pittsburgh. Baldwin Locomotive Works in Philadelphia built Engine 2472. The Philadelphia Phillies beat the Chicago Cubs 26-23. John Wanamaker, US merchant who founded a chain of stores in Philadelphia, died. Mennonites from Canada and Pennsylvania fled persecution and settled near Chihuahua, Mexico. The 18-story Philadelphia Inquirer building was completed as home for the Philadelphia Inquirer newspaper. First radio station begins to broadcast. Decline in trolley ridership began on both sides of the river. Dr. Albert C. Barnes built a mansion to house his collection of French art masterpieces in Merion. The Pottsville Maroons beat the Chicago Cardinals for the NFL championship, but lost it on a technicality. Gene Tunney defeated Jack Dempsey for the World Heavyweight Boxing championship in Philadelphia. Market Street Bridge widened from two lanes to four and part of the Capitol complex, State Street Bridge, built, in Harrisburg. The 1st armored commercial car hold-up in US took place in Pittsburgh. The Great Depression begins.

CHAPTER 3

Generation Three

Who we are cannot be separated from where we're from.
—MALCOLM GLADWELL

Our four grandparents, whose photographs adorn the front of this book, comprise the Third Generation and is the starting point for the detailed biographies included in this volume. To place them in understandable location and time, the following information was downloaded from our ancestry.com FTM file. This brief biographical information, and the historical text that follows, will allow the reader to not only identify the starting point of the following biographies, but also allow a better understanding of the times, places and events.

HARPER BRUCE THOMPSON
& MYRTLE ADELINE BATDORF

Paternal Grandfather: Harper Thompson was born on September 28, 1907 in Sheridan, Schuylkill County, Pennsylvania to Abel & Gussie Thompson. Harper was counted in the census in 1910 in Porter, Schuylkill County, Pennsylvania. He was counted in the census in 1920 in Porter, Schuylkill County, Pennsylvania. He was employed as a Boxer about Abt. 1929. He lived in Emmaus, Lehigh County, Pennsylvania in 1930. He was employed as a Lineman, Telephone Co in 1930. He and Myrtle were married on June 15, 1935 in St. John's Lutheran, Berrysburg, Dauphin County, Pennsylvania. He was counted in the census in 1940 in Tower City, Schuylkill County, Pennsylvania. He was employed as a Lineman, Bell Telephone Co in 1940. He died on July 23, 1981 in Polyclinic Hospital, Harrisburg, Dauphin County, Pennsylvania. His funeral was in 1981 in Jesse H Geigle, 2100 Linglestown Rd., Harrisburg, Dauphin County, Pennsylvania. He was buried in 1981 in Woodlawn Memorial Gardens, Harrisburg, Dauphin County, Pennsylvania.

Paternal Grandmother: Myrtle Batdorf was born on January 05, 1918 in Big Run, Dauphin County, Pennsylvania to James & Beulah Batdorf. Myrtle was baptized on October 11, 1918 in Evangelical Lutheran Circuit, Lykens, Dauphin County, Pennsylvania. She was counted in the census in 1920 in Washington, Dauphin County, Pennsylvania. She was counted in the census in 1930 in Lykens, Dauphin County, Pennsylvania. She was counted in the census in 1940 in Tower City, Schuylkill County, Pennsylvania. Her religious affiliation was Lakeside Lutheran Church. She died on May 08, 1983 in Polyclinic Hospital, Harrisburg, Dauphin County, Pennsylvania. Her funeral was in 1983 in Jesse H Geigle, 2100 Linglestown Rd., Harrisburg, Dauphin County, Pennsylvania. She was buried on May 11, 1983 in Woodlawn Memorial Gardens, Harrisburg, Dauphin County, Pennsylvania. Her estate was probated in May 1983 in Harrisburg, Dauphin County, Pennsylvania.

IRVIN DUNCAN &
MAMIE LUCETTA ANDERSON

Maternal Grandfather: Irvin Duncan was born on November 27, 1901 in Sunbury, Northumberland County, Pennsylvania to William & Lottie Duncan. Irvin was counted in the census in 1910 in Sunbury, Northumberland County, Pennsylvania. He was counted in the census in 1920 in Sunbury, Northumberland County, Pennsylvania. He and Mamie were married on June 07, 1926 in Sunbury, Northumberland County, Pennsylvania. He was counted in the census in 1940 in Hummels Wharf, Snyder, Pennsylvania. He was employed as a Proprietor of Retail produce in 1940 in Hummels Wharf, Snyder, Pennsylvania. He died on April 08, 1978 in Geisinger Medical Center, Mahoning, Montour County, Pennsylvania. His funeral was on April 11, 1978 in M. Quay Olley Funeral Home, 539 Race St., Sunbury, Northumberland County, Pennsylvania. He was buried on April 11, 1978 in Pomfret Manor Cemetery, Sunbury, Northumberland County, Pennsylvania.

Maternal Grandmother: Mamie Anderson was born on April 11, 1908 in Mother's home, Sunbury, Northumberland County, Pennsylvania to William & Emma Anderson. Mamie was counted in the census in 1910 in Sunbury, Northumberland County, Pennsylvania. She was counted in the census in 1920 in Monroe, Snyder County, Pennsylvania. She was employed as a Silk Mill about Abt. 1935. She was counted in the census in 1940 in Hummels Wharf, Snyder, Pennsylvania. She died on April 03, 1989 in Derry, Montour County, Pennsylvania. Her funeral was in 1989 in VL Seebold, 601 N High St, Selinsgrove, Snyder County, Pennsylvania. She was buried on April 05, 1989 in Pomfret Manor Cemetery, Sunbury, Northumberland County, Pennsylvania. Her estate was probated on February 05, 1990 in Montour County, Pennsylvania.

CURRENT EVENTS FOR OUR FOUR GRANDPARENTS

The Ford Model T of 1908 was the first automobile mass produced on assembly lines with completely interchangeable parts. It was the automobile that opened up travel to the common middle-class. The innovation of the assembly line was revolutionary.

World War I, beginning in 1914, was a conflict involving most of the world's powers. The beginning of the war was sparked by the assassination of Archduke Franz Ferdinand of Austria Hungary. The world quickly formed into alliances, The Allied Powers—United Kingdom, France, The Russian Empire, and later the United States—fought against the Central Powers—The German Empire, The Austro-Hungarian Empire, The Ottoman Empire and the Kingdom of Bulgaria. Over 70 million military personnel fought in the war including 60 million Europeans. The Western Front consisted of a trench line that changed little until 1917. More than 15 million people were killed; making World War I one of the deadliest conflicts in history.

The Great Depression was a worldwide economic downturn that started with the stock market crash of 1929. The depression varied in countries around the world but generally started in 1929 and lasted until the beginning of World War II. Unemployment rose to 25% in the US and as high as 33% in other countries. Countries whose jobs primarily came from industry suffered the most. The Great Depression was the largest economic downturn in history.

The Holocaust refers to the systematic genocide of over six million European Jews by Nazi Germany. The genocide began in stages in the early 1930's by removing Jews from society; moving the Jews to concentration camps, where they died of slave labor and disease; moving Jews to ghettos; mass shootings in conquered territories; and finally extermination camps where most Jews who survived the journey were killed in gas chambers.

World War II began on September 1, 1939 with the German invasion of Poland. The war involved most of the world's powers and was divided into two sides: the Allies versus the Axis. World War II changed the boundaries of war with significant actions against civilians including the Holocaust and the only use of nuclear weapons in war. 100 million military personnel were involved in the conflict. World War II was the deadliest war in history with over 70 million casualties. World War II ended in 1945 with the victory of The Allies.

CHAPTER 4

Generation Four

*We need to haunt the house of history
and listen anew to the ancestors' wisdom.*
—MAYA ANGELOU

Our Fourth Generation includes Abel and Gussie Thompson, James and Beulah Batdorf, William and Lottie Duncan and William and Emma Anderson, of the late 1880's in Pennsylvania.

ABEL ROBERT THOMPSON
& GUSSIE MAE HENSEL

Abel Robert Thompson came into this world on the eve of another cold Pennsylvania winter. He was born on November 28, 1880, to proud parents, Robert Bruce Thompson and Lydia Ann Goodman both Pennsylvania natives living in Sheridan at the time. Carrying on the family tradition of honoring their ancestors, Abel bore the middle name Robert, his father's name. Abel's family had a long and important history in the area where he was born and grew up. The town of Sheridan was laid by his grandfather, Alexander Thompson, on his former lands. Grandfather Alexander was the first to sell coal from the area, later known as the York Farm Colliery, and Alexander was the owner of Thompson's Mill.

Just two days after the celebration of St. Valentine's Day, February 16, 1885, an adorable baby girl was born to Howard Andrew Carson Hensel and Clara Matilda Updegrove. She was baptized Augusta Mae on April 5, 1885, in Dauphin County, Pennsylvania. Gussie, as she was fondly known, grew up during the staunch age of Victorianism. She was able to attend school only until the fifth grade. Being the oldest of eleven children, her formal education was cut short when it became necessary for Gussie to begin assisting in the household duties and the care of her siblings. With so many mouths to feed in the family, it was later necessary for her to become an additional bread winner—as a teen, she was employed as a domestic servant. However, it wouldn't be long before she would move on to married life.

When Gussie met Abel, he was working as a general laborer. He was a tall, handsome man with dark hair, grey eyes, and a lean physique from the efforts of his occupation. Gussie never had eyes for any other man. She was a lovely June bride dressed in flowing white when the two married on June 15, 1904, in Schuylkill County, Pennsylvania. The new couple was soon expecting their first child. However, their joy turned tragic when their baby daughter, Virginia, died not long after she was born. A son, Wilbur Clark, came along in 1906, and a second son, Harper Bruce, was born in September of 1907. Now with two children, Abel sought to better his financial position. His uncle, the Honorable Alexander F. Thompson, had been a member of the Dauphin County bar and served as a state senate member. These political connections may have led to Abel's position as a probationer with the local courts.

By 1910, the couple had been married for six years and was well settled in Porter Township. Schuylkill County would soon be celebrating its centennial and nearby Pottsville was a growing mini-metropolis with ample educational opportunities for neighboring children. Abel had decided to return to the family roots and had been working as a coal miner for eight years. Perhaps the coal miners' strike of 1902, which ended with shorter work days and 10% pay increases after President Theodore Roosevelt's successful arbitration, played a role in Abel taking up mining. Soon, he and Gussie had saved enough to purchase their own home. They were even able to rent space in the household to a small family. Gussie was expecting their fourth child, Abel Franklin, who would be born in October 1910. Their daughter, Lydia Mae, would follow in February four years later.

With a growing family, Abel sensed the increased responsibility that came with it. His job as a miner was fraught with peril—it was all too often he heard of explosions, cave-ins, or exposure to deadly mine gasses. These dangers were impressed upon him by the 1892 explosion at York Farm Colliery—when he was eleven years old—that killed fifteen men. The Molly Maguires, a society of activists who fought to improve the dangerous working conditions in the mines, had actively campaigned for better working conditions, but positive changes were still some time off. Violent clashes between organized workers and mine bosses continued throughout Abel's life, from the hanging of twenty Pennsylvania coal miners believed to be members of the Molly Maguires in the 1870s and the Lattimer Massacre in nearby Hazleton in 1897, to the infamous Ludlow Massacre and ensuing Colorado Coalfield War, in which hundreds died in that very year of 1914. Realizing both the apparent and unseen dangers of his profession, Abel took no chances in providing for his family should some ill-fated event occur. He filed his will at the local courthouse in Porter on July 2, 1914.

Abel was obviously pondering the future when he filed his will. Perhaps it was a general sense of foreboding, or maybe he had the feeling that something just wasn't quite right. One of the unseen dangers of a coal miner's life was black lung, always a concern for both current and former miners. Or perhaps it was his plans for an adventurous trip to Colorado. Whatever the case, he was wise to plan well.

Abel heard of the mining booms taking place in Colorado. Family stories say that he left Pennsylvania in search of copper in Colorado. Although copper mines were scarce in Colorado, swindlers like the notorious W. C. Calhoun were not. Abel could have met or heard about Calhoun and the copper mine stocks he was selling. Wanting to provide for his wife and new children, Abel may have left for Colorado to check on his investments; or maybe it was the adventurous spirit instilled in Abel by his grandfather, Alexander, who left Scotland to come to the New World. Upon his arrival in Colorado, Abel found that his stocks were potentially fraudulent and took up employment in one of the many booming gold or silver mines of the time. Gussie, a resourceful woman, was left at home to care for their children.

Abel's trip to Colorado left him feeling rather unwell and he had a strong yearning to return home to familiar soil. Shortly thereafter, he became a victim of the influenza pandemic, and after contracting pneumonia, he died on October 15, 1918. He was just 37 years of age. The leaves had begun to fall, and the Pennsylvanian mountains were awash with beauty and color. The family gathered for Abel's burial services on a windswept October day. They said their final goodbyes as he was returned to the soil so near to where his life had begun. His mortal remains were laid to rest in Greenwood Cemetery in Tower City, Pennsylvania.

Abel died leaving Gussie with four small children all under the age of twelve. Rather than choosing to remarry, Gussie decided to brave the world on her own. Luckily, the family home had already been paid for so she and the children had a secure roof over their heads. Gussie's lack of education left her with few options for income, but this did not hinder her in finding a way to earn much-needed funds. With her agile hands, she found plenty of work as a seamstress. This allowed her to remain at home and tend to her children while also supporting the family financially. The boys were still attending school and too young to contribute to the family income, but they managed to persevere and remain together as a family through this trying period of their lives.

In just a decade, Gussie was a financially stable widow living in a community among many other widows. It was a coming new age of amazing technologies. Advances in aviation allowed the imagination to take flight by following the travels and tragedies of Amelia Earhart and Charles Lindbergh. The Jazz age was in full swing, and for a few hard-earned pennies, one could enter the strange and wonderful world of The Wizard of Oz, a moving picture show. Gussie was likely amazed at seeing so many things she never could have dreamed of at the turn of the century.

Still the family prevailed as a whole. Gussie was fortunate to be keeping house for her children well away from the Midwestern Dust Bowl and they were lucky enough to be among those who still had jobs at the beginning of the Great Depression. The boys were working as coal miners and Lydia had begun her long-term job as a looper at a hosiery factory. Even for those in a household with multiple incomes, the nation's financial situation dictated frugality in all things. Radio was gaining popularity as an economic American pastime. Like many other families who owned a radio set, Gussie and her children probably spent the evenings listening to their favorite broadcast programs. A pleasant accompaniment would have been a fresh-baked plate of the newly invented Toll House chocolate chip cookies and fresh milk all around.

Several years later, Gussie and Lydia were still living on Main Street in Sheridan. It was a middle-class neighborhood populated mostly by miners and mill workers. Gussie was surely proud to own her home at a value of $680, which would be equal to about $11,315 today. She took care of the house while Lydia worked at the stocking mill. Being the highest paid looper in the area, Lydia earned $550 a year to support them both. It was a modest lifestyle when a loaf of bread cost about eight cents, a quart of milk averaged eleven cents, and eggs were nearly 27 cents a dozen. With a little more than $10 a month to live on, economizing was a continuing necessity.

While the radio was one of the main leisure activities available, it was also the main means of getting the news. When Germany invaded France and Italy declared war on Britain and France, it no doubt caused them much concern. It was the beginning of a period of unrest that would last for many years. The loss and devastation of WWII may have been the catalyst for Gussie to face her own eventual mortality. She filed her last will and testament at the local courthouse on May 27, 1950, not long after her 65th birthday, at which point she would have started drawing on her Social Security benefits, another innovation of the 20th century.

It would be several more decades before the reading of Gussie's will would come to pass. During that time, she continued to live with and keep house for Lydia, who never married. She continued to find comfort in Lydia's countenance, which reminded her of the dear husband so many years gone. Living through these years, she would see many changes in youth morality, racial discrimination, and in the political face of America. She would experience the loss of her son Wilbur Clark, who left behind a widow, Elva May.

Gussie, an aging widow with a childhood rooted in the Victorian age, took these changes in stride. She occupied her time in charitable efforts as a member of the Women's Society of Christian Service. Finding a commonality amongst other Methodist ladies of similar age and like mind, she spent her days in Bible study fellowship, sharing the gospel with others, aiding the poor, visiting the aged, and assisting those of general misfortune. When she was not on her missions as benefactor, she practiced her faith at the Lykens United Methodist Church or the Wesley United Methodist Church in Tower City. It was a faith that Gussie continued to practice until her passing in March of 1973.

Gussie Hensel Thompson departed this world at the respectable age of eighty-eight years. Her heart and circulatory system failing, she experienced a brain hemorrhage and breathed her last breath peacefully at home on March 27, 1973. It was a chilly day when her loved ones attended her funeral services at the Dean O. Snyder Mortuary in Tower City. There to pay respects were her sons Abel Franklin and wife, Almeda Ellen; Harper Bruce and wife, Myrtle Adeline; and of course, her faithful daughter, Lydia Mae. She was laid to rest next to her beloved Abel in Tower City's historic Greenwood Cemetery. Buried amongst many family and friends, their place of committal is a peaceful memorial garden overlooking a meandering branch of the great Schuylkill River. Abel and Gussie's third child, Harper, was the direct ancestor of the Thompson line.

JAMES EDWARD BATDORF
& BEULAH IRENE WERT

Having been born in Loyalton, Dauphin County, Pennsylvania, in 1885, James Edward Batdorf had little control over his fate. In an area where nearly all employment was tied directly or indirectly to the world's largest deposits of anthracite coal, he became a coal miner. Loyalton is an unincorporated community within Washington Township and it's likely that James went to one of the nine one-room schoolhouses in Washington Township, and dropped out after the equivalent of eighth grade to go to work. According to a 1900 Bureau of Mines report, 363 collieries in the anthracite region employed 143,826 workers, one-fourth of them boys under the age of sixteen.

Though deep-mining anthracite coal was tough and dangerous work—anthracite mine accidents in Eastern Pennsylvania in 1900 killed 411, injured 1,057, and made 230 widows and 525 orphans—it also offered substantial pay. A certified miner could earn twice the national average 1910 pay of $750 a year. To be certified, a miner had to pass a test in English, buy his own tools and equipment, and hire his own laborers or, as they were called, butties.

Anthracite is the highest grade of coal in the earth. Anthracite burns cleaner, hotter, and four times longer than bituminous and is virtually smoke free, while bituminous combustion emits a sooty black smoke. The anthracite coal mined in Eastern Pennsylvania fueled iron blast furnaces for the production of high-grade steel, drove railroads, and heated homes. The U.S. Navy especially coveted anthracite. The heat gave warships speed and the lack of smoke gave them stealth.

At 5'6" and about 145 pounds as an adult, James Batdorf was an ideal size for deep mining work. He was a family man, good friend, and a public servant. In January of 1906, when he was nineteen, he went to the state capital of Harrisburg to be a pallbearer for a family friend of his sister Frances's finance Samuel Lutz. In August of that year James attended the marriage of his sister and Lutz in his parents' home, where he still lived. Pastor Brown of the Evangelical Church performed the wedding of Frances and Samuel and they departed immediately to honeymoon in Atlantic City.

James and Frances were two of seventeen children born to Thomas and Mary Louisa Peters Batdorf, both of whom were born in Dauphin County, Pennsylvania. Thomas was the descendant of Batdorfs who were among the Palatines, so-called because they emigrated from Palatinate, a region in southwestern Germany, due to economic devastation and religious persecution following the Thirty Years War that occurred from 1618 to 1638 in Central Europe, Those immigrants spoke a German dialect that became the Pennsylvania Dutch language still spoken today by the Amish.

Four of Thomas and Mary's children—Alvin, George, Kirby, and Norman—died in childhood. The other twelve—Verna, Stella, Cora, Harvey, Joseph, Frances, Oscar, James, Adam, Mary Ellen, William, and John—lived into adulthood.

In 1908, James, twenty-three, married Beulah Wert, nineteen. Though James, as his father had, went by his middle name Edward in his day-to-day life, when he was mentioned in local newspapers, such as when he ran as a Republican for inspector of elections in 1917, he was always James. James and Beulah settled in Washington Township to live next to her parents—John Wert, born in neighboring Northumberland County, and Adeline Row, born in Dauphin County.

In the 1910 census the Werts and Batdorfs lived right next door to one another. The 1920 census shows both families moved to State Road in Washington Township, and again James and Beulah lived next door to her parents' home, which was described as a farm. The 1920 census also shows John and Adeline had a grandson, John Schiffer, living with them. As James and Beulah had five of their eventual six children by then—Alvin Leroy, Margaret Irene, Mildred Catherine, Harry Franklin and Myrtle Adeline—it's likely they moved to a bigger home. Romaine came later. James and Beulah were counted in the 1930 and the 1940 census, having moved to Lykens Borough, adjacent to Washington Township.

Beulah was born in 1889 in Elizabethville, just five miles southwest of Loyalton, where James was born. Both towns are in the Lykens Valley between the Mahantango and Berry ranges of the Appalachian Mountain range, an idyllic setting of rolling pastures and quaint towns set off by green mountains turning red and gold in the fall and gradually climbing to 1,500 to 2,000 feet.

Beulah was the fifth of six siblings of John and Adeline Row Wert, coming after Caroline, Harriet, a third child about whom little is known, and Florence. Beulah was the fifth child, followed by her sister Margaret. Beulah's work ethic was as strong as her husband's. She did most of the child rearing, kept the house, worked the family's garden, and was also a skilled dressmaker. In 1950, at the age of sixty-one, she was working hanging wallpaper.

Growing industries, railroads, and WWI kept the demand for coal high during the 1910s and 1920s—thus James and Beulah thrived. About 1922, the family bought its first automobile, a Ford Model T. They found plenty of recreation in the Lykens Valley with home-based card parties, church picnics, hiking clubs, and colliery competitions with baseball and tug of war games. Visiting family and friends was a pastime. The area was well connected by rail and in 1911, when James's brother Harvey visited his parents at Elizabethville, it was a news item in the Harrisburg Patriot's Nearby Towns section. A card party held by a Beatrice Batdorf at Lykens was also news.

Baseball and bowling were popular pastimes. Lykens and Elizabethville both had teams in the Twin County baseball league. A man named Batdorf, no first name given, was one of the top bowlers in the Allison Hill league. An F. Batdorf played basketball for the Wiconisco High School team in the early 1920s. It is not known if James was a ballplayer or bowler, but it's likely he participated in colliery games

When the anthracite industry waned in the 1930s due to the Depression, James continued working as a road construction laborer with the Work Progress Administration and later for Lykens Borough, and was still working when he died in 1954 at age sixty-nine. Beulah survived him by twenty-nine years, living to her late nineties. They are buried side by side at Calvary United Methodist in Wiconisco.

Notes taken by Marc D. Thompson during an interview with James' and Beulah's daughter Mildred when she was eighty-eight gives a glimpse of what life was like in the Lykens Valley during part of James' and Beulah's life:

Mildred was born Mildred Catherine Batdorf on January 29, 1911, the daughter of Beulah Wert and James "Edward" Batdorf. She was the sister of my grandmother Myrtle, Alvin, Margaret, Harry, Ruth, and Romaine. Mildred and Myrtle were born and raised in Big Run, Pennsylvania. Their mother, Beulah, was the daughter of John and Adaline Wert of Big Run. The Wert family farmed and "were hard-working people." James Edward was the son of Thomas and Mary Batdorf, also of Big Run. Their "grandmother Batdorf was a housewife and grandfather Batdorf was a farmer and worked in the mines." Myrtle and Mildred "lived in a two-story house and ate in the kitchen." Their home was heated by coal and they did not have a fireplace. The family did not always have electricity, as candles, kerosene, and coal were used. The home had a cellar and water was retrieved from a well. Mail was delivered by rural route and they "had a cat named Blacky." Mildred was the fourth child born and Myrtle was the youngest of the seven children. As children, their major chore, among others, was doing the dishes. Their mother did the cooking and ironing and she taught them to sew, crochet, knit, and embroider. Mildred learned to drive a car from a neighborhood boy and her husband, Randall Moon, taught her to cook. Mildred and Myrtle's father, Edward Batdorf, was a miner and Mildred worked to help contribute to the family income. She was fourteen years old when she secured her first job. The family had a garden and they "dug the ground and got it ready to plant. They grew potatoes, lettuce, celery, onions, tomatoes, peppers, cabbage and a lot more." They had cherry and peach trees. Their mother did canning and raised chickens and the family often ate beef, pork, and chicken. Her parents and siblings did all the work, hiring no one to help with the house, garden, or animals. "Saturday was the day that you got a rest for the weekend and Sunday we got ready for church." The family attended a small church in Loyalton. For Christmas they would wake up early to see the tree and they received clothes as gifts. On July Fourth, "my brother had a birthday and we had games that we played." In general, however, sibling's birthdays were just another day. For her birthday, Mildred received clothes made by her mother. The family did not entertain often but they did go to family picnics. Mildred kept in touch with distant family and visited relatives often. In the summer, "we sat under a nice shade tree to keep cool" and in the winter kept warm with long johns. Mildred recalls one extreme winter storm when the snow reached up over the fences. For recreation, the children played jump rope, ball and cards. Mildred's best friend was Hilda Buffington and they often played games for fun. Mildred did not learn to swim and the family never went on vacation. Growing up, there was no place to shop so the family ordered items from "men who came around and the next day he came with it." They never went to the city to shop but there was a small country store. Lykens was the largest town nearby and Mildred used to take the train to visit her grandmother in Elizabethville. My father "got a car when I was ten years old. It was a Ford model T." Mildred attended a little red one-room schoolhouse in Big Run. It was only two houses away and she usually walked to school alone. Mildred was closest to her mother and she admired her father most. When young, Mildred "hoped to be a good housekeeper." Her family supported and encouraged her and they influenced her and helped her develop skills. When asked if she would choose the same career path, she said, "No. I would choose for a better life." "I met my husband in Lykens. I was engaged on Easter and married on October 1, 1926." Mildred was married in Hagerstown to her husband, a dentist, and her children were born in Pennsylvania.

They likely did not have electricity for the first twenty-five years of their marriage, because as late as 1936, 75 percent of Pennsylvania farms were not electrified. So they used candles and lanterns for nighttime light, heated with coal, and fetched water from a well. The family kept a garden—really a small truck farm—growing potatoes, lettuce, celery, onions, tomatoes, peppers, and cabbages, cherry and peach trees, and raising chickens, cows, and hogs. The children were expected to help with chores, and by the age of fourteen or so, they were getting their first jobs and contributing to the family's expenses. Myrtle, the direct ancestor of the Thompson line, grew up and went to school in the very small town of Big Run.

WILLIAM DUNCAN &
CHARLOTTE VIRGINIA LAYMAN

William Duncan, the eldest son of Fredrick and Catherine Duncan, was born in January 1876 in Sunbury, Pennsylvania. He was baptized that same year at the Zion Evangelical Lutheran Church. The building that housed the church was built in 1803 with the help of another similar but decidedly different religion, the German Reformed Church. The two denominations shared the building and its 65-acre grounds for almost 100 years. It would later be known as the Stone Valley Church.

William grew up in Sunbury with his two older sisters, Melinda and Sallie, and was followed by three more siblings, Gerty, Lilly, and Charley. Being the oldest boy, William probably preferred to follow his father as a laborer, but settled into the blacksmith trade. William was working as a blacksmith's apprentice when he met Charlotte Virginia Layman, called Lottie by her family and friends. The two were married in 1899—he was 23 and she was 20.

The following year, William started his own blacksmith business, but the business was short- lived as the Industrial Age made small blacksmithing enterprises all but obsolete. By the late 1800s, the railroads had linked the country and hardware was manufactured at plants and sold in hardware stores. In 1901, William was a laborer, possibly in the rail yards.

This may have been where William heard of the mining booms taking place in Colorado. Family stories say that William left Sunbury in search of copper in Colorado. This could be possible. Although copper mines were scarce in Colorado, swindlers like the notorious W. C. Calhoun were not.

Working on the railroad in Sunbury, William could have met or heard about Calhoun and the copper mine stocks he was selling. Calhoun was reportedly selling these stocks in 1900 and 1901 before the Copper Mining Syndicate Ltd he was associated with folded in April 1901. Wanting to provide for his wife and new son, Irvin Wilfred Duncan—born November 27, 1901—may have left for Colorado to check on his investments; or maybe it was the adventurous spirit instilled in William by his father, Fredrick, who left Germany to come to the New World.

Regardless of the reason, there is no documentation of William residing in

Pennsylvania from 1902 to 1905. Reported by Irvin in his later years, this is the time that William was in Colorado. Upon arrival in Colorado, William found that his stocks were potentially fraudulent and took up employment in one of the many booming gold or silver mines of the time. Lottie, a resourceful woman, was left in Sunbury to care for her baby. This resilience may have come from her upbringing.

Lottie was the second of fourteen children born to Joseph Layman and Rebecca Overlander Layman. Lottie was born on May 12, 1879 in Brogueville, York County, Pennsylvania. At that time in history, Brogueville was largely a lush agricultural area of mainly wheat and tobacco. It is speculated that Joseph may have been a farmer of one or both of these crops. Being the second of fourteen children, Lottie was undoubtedly depended upon to look after her younger siblings and probably worked on the family farm as well. These experiences at such a young age almost certainly taught her confidence and self-reliance.

It is not known what exactly brought the Layman family to Sunbury, but it may have been the devastating flood of 1884. A rainstorm started on the night of June 25 and lasted until about three a.m. the next morning. A record twelve inches of rain fell in just over seven hours.

The devastation was realized the next morning when the Codorus Creek, usually about 85 feet wide, was now one-quarter of a mile wide. Bridges and train tracks were washed away, debris from up the stream—buildings, farming implements, furniture, dead and living animals—were seen in the passing waters. The cost of repairs to the county exceeded $700,000 with $91,000 just in temporary bridges. In today's terms that would equal approximately $956,000,000.

Or maybe it was the surprise of the earthquake that rocked York County only two months later in August that prompted Joseph to move his family to what he perceived was a safer place. Either way, the Layman family pulled up stakes in Brogueville and moved to Sunbury, Pennsylvania.

That being said, any or all of these incidences probably lead to Lottie's confidence in taking care of herself and her son in the absence of her husband. One of the ways she took control of her life was to take in boarders. One such boarder was George Glace, a 21-year-old gentleman who worked as a weaver in the textile industry in Sunbury.

A few years after leaving for the Colorado mines, William returned to his family, unfortunately very sick with what was believed to be pulmonary tuberculosis, probably contracted while working in the Colorado mines. William worked for a short period as a machinist, probably for the railroad, before his death in September 1906.

Once again Lottie was left to care for her son, now age five. Shortly after William's death, Lottie married William H. McNutt, a gentleman five years her junior. We don't know how their marriage terminated, possibly his young years or inexperience left him unable to deal with the bond that she shared with the real love of her life—her son, Irvin—and he just left. We don't have a divorce or death certificate for the younger William, only speculation.

About 1920 Lottie remarried another William—William Grant Willard. They were married for thirteen years. William had nine children with his first wife, Elizabeth, who died in 1916; he brought five of these children into his marriage with Lottie.

The blending of the two families did not go well and Irvin was ostracized by his stepbrothers and stepsisters. He was eighteen at the time of the marriage and probably moved out on his own. However, Lottie and Irvin's relationship went unrivaled and Irvin remained the main man in her life. In 1933, the third William passed away.

At some point after the death of her third husband, Lottie went to live with Irvin and his wife, Mamie. Lottie passed away in 1936 at their home in Monroe, Snyder County, Pennsylvania. William and Lottie's only child, Irvin, was the direct ancestor of the Thompson line.

WILLIAM ANDERSON
& EMMA LOUISE KEEFER

William Morris Anderson and Emma Louisa Keefer married in 1902 and were husband and wife for more than 60 years. They spent their entire lives within 50 miles of their birthplaces, and upon their deaths came to rest together in a local cemetery.

It made perfect sense to them that they would never move from the area as both of them came from families with very deep local roots. Their parents had all been born nearby, as had six of their eight grandparents.

Neither William nor Emma was highly educated, but they were physically strong, tireless, and determined to make a good life for themselves and for their children. They never felt entitled to "something for nothing." They were never wealthy in terms of possessions, but because they had worked for everything they had, they valued it all the more.

They took for granted that their commitment to each other was meant to last a lifetime. They were a devoted couple until Emma's death, at the age of eighty, in 1963. When William passed away eight years later, he was buried with Emma in Orchard Hill Cemetery in Shamokin Dam, Snyder County, Pennsylvania.

For his whole life, William made his living through the sweat of his brow and the effort of his strong arms. Emma worked hard too in a silk mill even before she was out of her teen years, as a housekeeper for pay in other people's homes, and—like nearly all the women she knew—as a mother and a wife. In an era when large families were the norm, Emma's growing brood of eight children was not unusual, except for one remarkable fact: her eight children included three sets of twins!

The Pennsylvania in which William and Emma lived their lives was known as the "most foreign" of the former American colonies. Unlike its neighboring colonies, Pennsylvania was founded by the Dutch not by the English. As a result of this history, it became a magnet for immigrants from German-speaking regions of Europe. More than 70 percent of immigrants to Pennsylvania before 1790 had been German, and German influence was still pervasive in rural areas such as Snyder, Northumberland, and Schuylkill counties.

Among the strong values the German immigrants had brought with them was their belief in education. As a result, Pennsylvania was one of the first states to pass a public education law. The Pennsylvania State Constitution of 1790 required free public education for children whose families could not afford to pay for schooling. However, despite the good intentions of the law, the development of public schools was slow, and it was only when William was fifteen years old—in 1895—that the state authorized every county to establish public high schools. Chances are that William and Emma's education ended before high school age, when they became old enough to begin to earn a living.

William was born on June 11, 1880, in McKees Half Falls in southeastern Pennsylvania's Snyder County. He was the son of James M. Anderson and Lucetta Gaugler, both of whom had been born in Snyder County. William had one older brother, Charles, and he was followed by Theodore, Thomas, Amy, Josephine, and Catherine.

Emma came along two years later on March 31, 1882, in the town of Ashland, two counties to the east in Schuylkill County. Her parents were James Pollock Keefer, who was born in Northumberland County, Pennsylvania, and Emma Louisa Livezly, born in Schuylkill County. Emma was named for her own mother, who died four days after baby Emma's birth. Curiously, Emma's paternal grandmother, Margaret Matilda Keefer, is the only relative who seems to have been present at Emma's baptism, which took place at the local Zion Evangelical Lutheran Church. After her mother Emma's death at age eighteen and her father's death ten years later, young Emma relocated to her paternal grandparents' home in Sunbury, Pennsylvania until she met and wed William.

By the time they were out of their teens, William had temporarily moved one county to the east and Emma had moved one county to the west. It was there, in Northumberland County, where they met and married.

William grew to 5 foot 7 inches tall, an average height for a man in those days, and he was strong and sturdy. His dark hair and blue eyes must have been attractive to Emma, and his strong work ethic would have suggested that he make be a good life partner.

At the time of their marriage on July 19, 1902, William was employed as a woodworker and Emma was a winder in a local silk mill. William later joined Emma in the local Northumberland County textile industry working as a laborer in a Sunbury dye works. By the turn of the century, synthetic dyes had largely replaced natural dyes. A dye works, in which raw threads and fabrics were colored, would have been a hot, backbreaking place to work.

Within a few years, though, the Andersons had moved their growing family across the Susquehanna River into Snyder County, a rural region of rolling hills and flat creek valleys, nearly all in farms or forests. In those days, most local residents made their living as farmers through harvesting and milling the hardwoods and softwoods of the forests, or on the railroad. At one time or another during his life, William tried his hand at every one of the region's primary economic enterprises. He had been a woodworker in Northumberland County, then he went to work for the railroad, and within a few more years he would become a one of the nation's several million small farmers.

In those decades, the Pennsylvania Railroad was a powerful wealthy enterprise. Laying track throughout the state to serve the state's coal mines and moving goods and passengers, it had an overstated influence in Pennsylvania State politics. Highly skilled railroad workers—such as locomotive engineers—were well-paid but common laborers who worked in dangerous exhausting jobs for very low wages. For a few years, William was one of these hard-working, poorly paid men.

During the 1920s, he tried his hand at farming, but it was a difficult time in America to be a farmer. America had suffered recession and depression in the aftermath of World War I, and though urban America had recovered, rural America suffered economically through the 1920s. Small farmers throughout America made do with very little money, though they were able to cushion themselves by raising most of their own food. When the Great Depression slammed rural America, however, the life of the small farmer became untenable and William had to find another line of work.

The New Deal's Works Progress Administration put millions of men to work as laborers in all parts of the nation. William was one of them, doing whatever he needed to do in order to care for his family. In addition to frequent jobs as a housekeeper, Emma kept busy as the mother of their eight children. The Andersons' first child, William Clemens, was born the year after their marriage. Next came Florence Violet.

Starting in 1908, Emma bore three sets of twins in a row. Charles Benton and Mamie Lucetta were born in 1908. This birth took place in the Andersons' house not in a hospital, which was typical for rural America in the early 1900s. It is likely that Emma's other births took place at home, too. Harvey Melvin and Harry Nevan were born next, with Donald Morris and David George completing the family. Remarkably, in those days before modern medicine, all eight children survived to adulthood.

During their lifetimes, from the 1880s to the 1960s, William and Emma witnessed astonishing technological advances in their world.

At the turn of the century, people's transportation choices had been limited to walking or riding steam-powered railroads and horse-drawn wagons. But in 1908, Henry Ford introduced the Model T—reliable, serviceable, and relatively affordable. A typical assembly-line worker could earn enough to buy a Model T in four months.[9] It would take longer for a farmer to earn enough to purchase an automobile or truck, but by the end of the 1920, even rural areas were connected by paved roads, with automobiles buzzing back and forth. We don't know when William and Emma first "got wheels," but it must have been an exciting day for the whole family!

The typical rural house in the 1880s lacked heating, electric lighting, and indoor plumbing. In fact, in 1925, of the 6.3 million farms in America, barely 200,000 had electric service. Beginning with the New Deal's Rural Electrification Act, the federal government began working with local authorities to bring electricity to rural areas like southeastern Pennsylvania. It is not known when William and Emma were first able to flip a switch and turn on a simple lightbulb, or when they were able to make a telephone call, or turn a tap, or flush a toilet, but by the end of their lives, the lack of these amenities was a distant memory. William and Emma's fourth child, Mamie—one of the sets of twins born in 1908—was the direct ancestor of the Thompson line.

CHAPTER 5

Generation Five

All the flowers of all the tomorrows are in the seeds of today.
—INDIAN PROVERB

Our Fifth Generation includes Robert and Lydia Thompson, Howard and Clara Hensel, Thomas and Mary Batdorf, John and Adeline Wert, Frederick and Catherine Duncan, Joseph and Rebecca Layman, James and Lucetta Anderson and James and Emma Keefer, of the mid 1880's in Pennsylvania and Germany.

ROBERT BRUCE THOMPSON
& LYDIA ANN GOODMAN

Named for his grandfather, Robert Bruce Thompson was delivered into this earthly world on September 24, 1847. The family gathered expectantly at their home on York Farm in Pottsville, Schuylkill County, Pennsylvania. The happy expectant parents, Alexander Thompson and Isabelle Stoddart Penman Thompson, eagerly awaited his arrival along with Robert's seven older brothers and sisters, George, Robert, David, William, Elizabeth, Janette, and Alexander. Robert was not the last child to be born to these parents—his younger siblings, Isabelle and James, would later follow.

Robert's early years were spent growing up on York Farm, where his father raised crops. His family was also known to sell coal from the site, which would later become the famous York Farm Colliery. But his carefree childhood existence would soon see many changes. In 1851, at only four years old, Robert would mourn the loss of his mother. It was the same year that Pottsville became the Schuylkill County seat. Three years later, the family would move to a 110-acre farm in the sparsely settled Porter Township area. The farm grew smaller as Robert grew older and the town of Sheridan grew around him. Robert would gain a stepmother when his father took Mary Bast as his new wife. Over the next several years, Robert would be joined by an additional twelve half-siblings as well. He was still living at home and working as a laborer in 1870.

Almost nine years after Robert was born, the Goodman family was expecting the birth of a child. Lydia Ann Goodman arrived on February 20, 1856, and was baptized the very same day. She was the tenth child born to Michael Goodman and his wife, Mary Magdalene Brown Goodman, of Clarks Valley, Dauphin County, Pennsylvania. Lydia grew up on a farm as well. Her youth was uneventful as her older brothers and sisters married and left the nest one by one. By 1870, her brother George was the only sibling remaining at home.

Lydia herself left the parental nest to marry Robert in 1873. She was a delicate young bride at just seventeen years of age. Her sisters Susan and Magdalena were probably on hand to give marital advice to the blushing bride as sisters Sarah and Anna helped Lydia into a crisp white dress accentuated with lace and bows. Dainty earrings adorned her lobes and her soft dark curls framed a face that showed both trepidation and bright expectation. Robert was fashionably dressed in a debonair suit. One could easily imagine the slight smile that played upon his lips as Lydia's brothers, William and John, took him aside for hearty congratulations. Clean shaven, dark hair slightly parted to the side, he faced his new bride with delight. Their wedding took place in Schuylkill County, Pennsylvania, and it was no doubt a grand affair. A jubilant celebration was held with many family members in attendance, including Lydia's brothers, Jacob and George.

Barely settled into married life, the newlywed couple was soon expecting their first child. A son, Benjamin, was born in 1874, but was lost to them in 1875, less than two years later. A second son, Oliver Charles, was born December 13, 1875, bringing a spark of Christmas joy and a measure of comfort for the grieving parents. The couple's only daughter, Laura Louisa, was born in March of 1878. Lydia and Robert were living in Rush Township, Dauphin County, Pennsylvania, when Abel Robert was born on November 28, 1880. Robert was working as a coal miner, probably at the Brookside Colliery in Tower City, where he had been employed for many years. Lydia's parents, Michael and Magdalena, were living next door.

Of course, their lives had not been without tragedy. Two of Robert's older brothers served in the Civil War. Alexander F. Thompson served three enlistments and survived to be a prominent attorney and state senator, but William W. Thompson died in 1862 to disease while serving in the Union Army. Robert's sister Elizabeth died while serving as a nurse during the war and a half-brother, Charles, was lost to a mining accident.

An even more personal tragedy struck in October of 1883, when Lydia and her infant son both passed. Little Franklin Henry was only eight weeks old and Lydia was barely over the age of 27, but age was not a discriminating factor. Without the benefit of hospital care, many new mothers died from complications of deliveries. Puerperal fever, a postpartum infection also known as childbed fever, was a very real threat. During her short life on this earth, Lydia was very well loved. Reverend Arthur Oakes presided with a comforting sermon, as many friends and family gathered close to aid Robert in his time of grief. As Robert was greatly respected, the funeral was the largest in the history of the town. The church overflowed with mourners, and the procession to the cemetery was long. Lydia and Franklin were buried together in Greenwood

Cemetery at Tower City, Schuylkill County, Pennsylvania on October 14, 1883.

Even with the support of family and friends, Robert took Lydia's death hard and became very ill. At the time, Robert was a member of the Patriotic Order Sons of America, probably at Washington Post 54 in Tower City. It was a fraternal group whose main goals were to support the public school system and to encourage patriotism and respect for the nation's heritage and Constitution. It was also their purpose to support fellow "brothers" in their hour of need. The group assisted with Lydia's funeral and stood by Robert, which greatly helped in his recovery.

Robert eventually regained his strength and began to rebuild his life. Rising to prominence in the area, Robert had taken a three-year position in the township government as a supervisor, which may have also included duties as a tax collector. He was fortunate enough to find love again with Mary Margaret Moser Uhler, a widow. The two would soon marry and have at least two children together. Their daughter, Agnes Ellen Lenora, was born in September 1888 in Tower City and baptized shortly thereafter. It is possible that they had another daughter named Lillie, but this may have simply been a nickname used by Agnes. Lillie married twice and had several children. She is buried in Greenwood Cemetery with her second husband, Charles Haubenstine. A son, Allen Herbert, was born in January 1891, in Tower City. He served in WWI and was a great source of pride for the family. He died in 1962 and is buried in Greenwood Cemetery along with other Thompson family members.

As if the loss of loved ones through illness and disease were not enough, fate would deal yet another blow to Robert. As he was returning from his job as Porter Township supervisor, his normally docile horse was spooked by a bicycle and bolted. Robert was thrown from his carriage and he sustained a severely broken leg that required hospital care. Had he landed on the other side of the road, he may have been thrown down a steep embankment and killed. It was a narrow escape from death.

Mortal peril would soon strike again. Robert had already lost a son to diphtheria when he himself was struck down by another terrible disease. While just as common and deadly a malady, typhoid fever was often transmitted through contaminated food or drinking water. It would claim Robert on October 10, 1907, one day after the 24th anniversary of Lydia's death. His burial took place in Greenwood Cemetery at Tower City on Sunday, October 13, 1907. With autumn leaves falling like the tears of those bereaved, Robert was finally at rest with his wife and children.

Several of Robert and Lydia's children were still living when Robert passed on. Oliver, who was born in Rush Township, rose to prominence in the community of Tower City. There he became the prosperous owner of the Mansion Hotel. He married Blanche Charlesworth, who was born in 1883 and who would die at age 32 in 1915. Laura Louisa would marry Charles McGough around 1903, and the couple would have several wonderful children. Appreciating the value of family, Laura remained close to her half-brother, Allen, for many years. Abel Robert would marry Augusta Mae "Gussie" Hensel on June 15, 1904. Robert and Gussie would have a short but happy life together. They had five children, four of whom lived to adulthood to carry on the Thompson family legacy, Abel Robert Thompson was the direct ancestor of the Thompson line.

See page 134 for photograph of Robert and Lydia Thomson.

HOWARD HENSEL &
CLARA MATILDA UPDEGROVE

In the summer of 1858, the Hensel family welcomed their fourth son and named him Howard Andrew Carson Hensel, after his father. His parents, Andrew Guise Hensel and Catherine Workman Hensel, and his two older brothers, Joseph and Ira, welcomed the new addition with joy and excitement to their home in Wiconisco, Pennsylvania. The eldest son, John Henry William, died as an infant, as was sadly common at the time.

The Reverend William Yose presided over Howard's baptism, and the neighbors and nearby cousins came to welcome the new baby. With three boys born within four years of one another, it was a busy household that would continue to grow. Over the next eight years, four daughters were added to the family: Catherine, Lillian, Clarissa, and Emma filled out a family of eight children.

In 1870, their father, Andrew, worked as a plasterer, helping to keep the ever-increasing number of miners in the region housed. In 1877, mother, Catherine, passed away, leaving the younger members of the family without a mother as they came of age. Howard was eighteen at that time and had likely already been working to help support the family. In 1880, he was still at home working as a laborer, helping his father to support his sisters while also saving for his own future.

In the same year that the Hensels welcomed their youngest daughter, the Updegrove family announced the birth of their second daughter, Clara Matilda, on November 30, 1866, in Lower Ranch Creek, Tremont, Pennsylvania. That December, she was baptized by Reverend Brady and introduced to the community. Her big sister, Anna, about two years old, was particularly proud. Her parents, Daniel Updegrove, a laborer and miner who was originally from Wiconisco, and Sarah Culp, from nearby Union County, would have two more children—William and Nora—in the following years.

Having likely met through one of Howard's co-workers, Howard and Clara took to each other quickly and were married after a brief courtship on his 26th birthday—September 2, 1884—surrounded by family and friends in Wiconisco. Howard's sisters, who were near to Clara's age, were buzzing with excitement for the event. His older brothers came to offer congratulations and advice. Naturally, Clara's sisters, Anna and Nora, were heavily involved in dressing and beautifying the bride. While the white dress had been popularized by Queen Victoria, middle- and working-class brides often chose more practical colors. Clara wore a dark brown and cream-colored dress with neat, modest embroidery and a high neck. This would be her best dress for formal occasions in the coming years. Similarly, Howard's new suit, tailored in dark brown to complement his wife's dress, would serve as his best attire for some time after the ceremony. A joyous wedding was held that Tuesday morning, followed by a wedding breakfast that gave time for congratulations and greetings. The young couple's neighbors wished them luck and fertility, and indeed Howard and Clara were blessed with both.

Clara was seventeen years old when she was married, and not long after her eighteenth birthday, on February 16, 1885, she gave birth to their first child, Augusta Mae, who would be known as "Gussie." The next year brought a son, Arthur. Then came two girls, Helen and Lillian, in 1888 and 1889, respectively. By 1890, Howard had four children to care for, and he had taken up coal mining, perhaps for higher wages than he could earn elsewhere as a laborer at that time. The family continued to grow as Elmer joined them in 1891, and both Myrtle and Clara were born in 1895. A third boy, Victor was born in 1897. The year 1899 brought a daughter, Virginia, into the fold.

At the turn of the century, Howard and Clara had nine children, all less than fifteen years of age. To help make ends meet, the eldest son, Arthur, was chipping in as a day laborer and coal miner at the age of thirteen. The family stepped into the next century boldly, bringing in a final son, Howard, and a final daughter, Edna, in 1902 and 1905. Eleven children made for a home more boisterous and busy than either parent had been brought up in, though only the younger six required much care. By the time Edna was born, the eldest five were old enough to take on jobs and responsibilities in the house to ease the burden on their parents.

At some point, Howard got out of the mines and into working with lumber. Perhaps the frequency of mining accidents, such as the 1892 explosion at nearby York Farm Colliery that killed fifteen men, or the periodic unrest over working conditions, or those poor conditions themselves, persuaded him to find a new line of work. By 1910, Howard had moved up to the position of engineer at a planing mill producing finished lumber, and his son Elmer was working at the same place as a carpenter. These jobs were less prone to disruptions in work than coal mining and were better paying as well. Having settled into a steady career as a skilled worker, Howard could look to the next decade with optimism.

By 1915, Howard had become a pillar of the community. Most of his eleven children were grown and beginning their own families, and he had reached the dignity that often comes to a man in his mid-fifties as his gray hair start to show. Similarly, Clara had grown from a blushing teenage bride to a loving grand-mother as she approached 50, still youthful but with more pronounced laugh lines. Howard took an active role in the local chapter of the Patriotic Order Sons of America, Washington Camp, encouraging patriotism and supporting public education. In those years of rapid immigration to America, such groups sought to help newcomers embrace their new home. He also accepted a position as dea-con for one of the several Methodist parishes in the area, taking part in the spir-itual education of his friends and neighbors.

Howard had a calling to save his brothers not only through Sunday services but also through practical action for workplace safety. In the 1920s, Howard branched out to firefighting—first in the coal mines, and later for Bestock Under-wear Mills in Tower City, Pennsylvania. In both the mining and the textile indus-tries, fire remained a constant danger. Having a long history of coal mining, Schuylkill County also had a rich history of volunteer firefighting companies to match, including more than 130 organizations over the years.

During the 1920s, Fords buzzed on the streets of the cities to the east and new electric refrigerators hummed in homes while fires roared in Appalachian coal country. The booming postwar economy had prompted the mining industry to expand, digging more and deeper mines and exposing larger than ever numbers of miners to various risks. Poorly ventilated mines were the primary cause as 597 Pennsylvania coal miners died in coal dust explosions during that decade—a larger toll than in the 1910s or 1930s. Larger mines required more non-mining work for safety measures such as ventilation. Consequently, the then-growing union movement continually struggled with the industry over safety provisions, making workers' health a primary concern. It stands to reason that as the nation turned its attention to industrial safety, local community leaders such as Howard were involved with hands-on implementation of important reforms that were needed in these increasingly mechanized workplaces.

In addition to prospering in the postwar economy, the Hensel family had been fortunate when it came to war. Both Howard and Clara's fathers had been mustered during the Civil War, and both returned home safely. Similarly, their luck held out when the States got involved in the First World War. The Hensels' immediate family did not suffer losses, but they undoubtedly were affected by the tragedies that befell their neighbors and friends during the war. They planted their Victory Garden, conserved their resources, and lent aid to their neighbors whose boys went off to war.

Rather, it was the following decade that would trouble the Hensels. Howard and Clara remained engaged as leaders within their community and family until Clara fell ill with cancer in the winter of her 59th year. She would not see her 60th birthday, succumbing on March 28, 1926. She was laid to rest in Greenwood Cemetery, Tower City, Schuylkill County, Pennsylvania, on March 31. Howard—and indeed the entire family— tried their best to adjust to life without the dear wife of 41 years and mother of eleven children. In the way that many lasting marriages end, Howard did not linger long before joining his wife in the afterlife the next year. The cause of death was determined to be arteriosclerosis, but perhaps loneliness was what really ailed his heart when he passed on June 6, 1927, at 68 years of age. On June 9, he was interred alongside his wife in Greenwood Cemetery.

The next generation of the Hensel family would have to weather the difficult years of depression and war that would soon follow without the guidance of their dear parents. While times were often challenging, the family would persevere. At this point, Gussie was a widow, having lost her husband, Abel Robert Thompson, in 1918. She was caring for her younger children and earning money as a seamstress. She likely took over as matron of the family, being the eldest of her generation.

Including Gussie's family of five children, Howard and Clara had a total of nineteen grandchildren. Daughter Gussie Hensel was the direct ancestor of the Thompson line.

See page 134 for photograph of Howard and Clara Hensel.

THOMAS EDWARD BATDORF
& MARY LOUISE PETERS

When Thomas Batdorf, named for his uncle Thomas Batdorf, was born to Peter Batdorf and Elizabeth Welker Batdorf in the Lykens/Big Run area of Dauphin County, Pennsylvania, in 1851, the United States of America was only seventy-five years old and Dauphin County, established in 1785, was only sixty-five years old.

Travel was by stagecoach, Conestoga wagon, canal, and ferry. Roads were dirt and, in the spring, nearly impassable mud, including the main road that connected Millersburg, Big Run, Lykens, and Elizabethville, and is Route 209 today.

The anthracite coal industry, which would dominate the economy in later years, was in its infancy in 1851, the coal having been discovered in 1825 and first shipped out of the area in 1834 to Millersburg by the Lykens Valley Railroad and Coal Company. At Millersburg, it was loaded on a Susquehanna River pole boat ferry. The railroad, which used horse power on a flat strip rail, was the fourth in the United States and the first in Dauphin County. Derailments were frequent and the 16-mile trip could take two days. Shipments stopped in 1845 when the railroad broke down until 1848 when the Wiconisco Canal was built and the railroad was improved with a T-rail. The coal was shipped as bulk ore until 1848 when the first coal breaker was built in Lykens.

With the coal industry just emerging in 1851 when Thomas was born, Dauphin County was virtually all rural and the economy depended on farming, hunting, fishing, and logging. Though much of the forests had been clear-cut for farms, buildings, heat, and lumber, perhaps 60 percent was still deeply wooded and home to pheasants, turkeys, deer, bear, and possibly even wolves and elk, though they were declining in Pennsylvania. The streams and lakes teemed with shad, salmon, and perch.6

By December 6, 1874, when Thomas married Mary Peters, much had changed. Thousands more acres had been clear-cut, roads improved, and passenger train service established. Berrysburg, Elizabethville, and Lykens were officially incorporated as boroughs.

As Thomas had been, Mary was born in Dauphin County. Her father was Samuel Peters, who had been born in Union County, and she was named after her mother, Mary Swartz, who had been born in Mifflin, a township in Juniata

County, the next county to the northeast of Dauphin County. Mary was the last of Samuel and Mary's seven children. Preceding her were John, Emma, Jonathan, Matthew, Matilda, and Jane.

Though Pennsylvania's 1790 state constitution had mandated free public primary education, few children in the Lykens/Elizabethville area went to school beyond the equivalent of seventh grade. Note that Mary was only sixteen when she married Thomas. Thomas also came from a large family, being the tenth of eleven children of Peter and Mary Louise. Thomas's older siblings were Esther, Jonas, Elizabeth, Susan, John, Sarah, Peter, Anna, and Rebecca, and he was followed by his sister Louisa.

After Thomas and Mary married, they settled in Elizabethville, where it is likely he was working in the mines, as the 1880 census shows his occupation as a laborer and the 1890 census shows him working as a miner. "Miner" was not a general term for mine workers, but rather a specific job that required certification. The 1910 census shows him as a retired laborer.

The 1870 census shows that four years before he married he was a blacksmith apprentice in Berrysburg to Henry Wise, twenty-four, who had a wife, Sarah, and a one-year old son, Charles. Thomas was a religious man. He was baptized in the German Reformed St. Peter's Church in Lykens and buried St. John's Evangelical Lutheran Cemetery in Loyalton when he died in 1916.

It is known that at least twice he attended the Pennsylvania Evangelical Conference in Berrysburg. In 1904 he attended with his wife and daughter Mary Ellen. In 1906 he attended with his wife, son Adam and daughter Frances.7

Thomas died at the age of sixty-five of heart and kidney disease. Mary survived Thomas by eight years, dying in 1924 of a cerebral hemorrhage. Mary Louisa Peters was buried on August 6, 1924, in St. John's Cemetery, Loyalton, from the Buffington Funeral Home. Before she married Thomas, she was counted in the census in 1860 and 1870 with her family in Mifflin and Washington Townships, Dauphin County. In 1880, 1890, 1900, and 1910 she was counted in Washington Township and Elizabethville with her husband. After his death, and four years before her death, she was counted in the census in 1920, still in Elizabethville, working as a housekeeper. Thomas and his siblings lived through famous historical events, including the violent United Mine Workers Strike of 1902—the only strike in which a sitting president, Theodore Roosevelt, intervened—and the Civil War.

Elizabethville was an important rail center during the Civil War. Men from the surrounding towns boarded trains there for Harrisburg to be mustered into the army. Among them was John Batdorf. Thomas, perhaps inspired by his older brother, though he was only fourteen in 1865 the last year of the war, lied about his age and enlisted. Unlike the five-foot-tall woman he would one day marry, Thomas was tall for his age, close to six feet. It was easy for the enlistment officers to believe he was eighteen, which was the age of enlistment. The Army did not require proof of age. They simply accepted.

While Thomas Batdorf, a man of family faith and country, and Mary Peters came from large families, their families were modest compared to the family they would create. They were the parents of seventeen children, born between the years of 1875 and 1899, a large family even by eighteenth century standards. Five of their children died in childhood, of those that lived into adulthood, their seventh child, James, is the direct ancestor of the Thompson line.

See page 136 for photograph of Thomas and Mary Batdorf.

JOHN H. WERT AND ADELINE ROW

John H. Wert was born in Dalmatia, Northumberland County, Pennsylvania, in 1855, the third of the eventual ten children of David M. Wert and Catherine Shoop. David's father was Jacob Wert. His mother was Sarah Faber. David was born on April 1, 1829, in Powell's Valley, Dauphin County. He was a farm laborer. John's mother, Catherine, was the daughter of John Shoop and Sarah Wertz. Catherine was born on February 24, 1830, in Northumberland County.8

John and older siblings Elizabeth and Anna were born in Northumberland County. His younger siblings, Mary, Melinda, Amelia, Daniel, and Isaac, were born after the family moved to adjacent Dauphin County, which was more prosperous than Northumberland.

John was working as a blacksmith in Washington Township, Dauphin County, when he met his wife, Adeline Row. Adeline was born in Dauphin County near Lykens borough on January 2, 1860. Her father was Daniel Row and her mother was Susan Frantz. Daniel was the son of John William Rowe and Barbara Rudy. He was born on July 10, 1813, in Dauphin County. Susan Frantz was born March 23, 1819, in Dauphin County. She was the daughter of Adam Frantz and Susan Gieseman.

Adeline was the youngest of seven siblings, following Sarah, Angelina, Adam, Susan, Amelia, and Leah. By 1870, the family had broken up. Adeline was living with her aunt, Susan Ely. Her father, Daniel, died on July 31, 1871, when Adeline was eleven.

John and Adeline married in 1878. She was eighteen, he was twenty-three. They wed in the "Church of the Hill," St. John's Lutheran Church. Built of stone on a hill overlooking the Lykens Valley in 1872, it replaced a log church built in 1802. The parish roots dated back to 1773 when the Reverend J. Enderline, a pioneer missionary, came to Lykens Valley.

John and Adeline settled in Washington Township, Dauphin County. By 1900, John had given up blacksmithing. The trade was in decline with the rise of factories, the development of the casting process, and less demand for horses in agriculture and transport. He became a freelance day laborer. That meant he was not on regular payroll of a farm or mine, but hired himself out on a daily basis where labor was needed. Since work was not steady, he needed help supporting his family. Adeline helped out running a farm on their property in Washington Township in the 1910s.

In 1879 they had a daughter, Caroline Wert. They eventually had five more children. Harriet was born in 1881. Another child, about whom little is known, was born in 1883. Florence was born on March 6, 1886. Beulah was born on New Year's Eve in 1889. Finally, Margaret was born in 1904.

John was a big man for the day at six-foot and a hard and willing worker. He coveted a union job with one of the coal companies. But in May 1902, United Mine Workers president John Mitchell organized an anthracite workers strike. In November of that year, U.S. President Teddy Roosevelt, fearing a shortage of coal for the winter, threatened to send in federal troops to take over the mines. Only then did the sides agree to end the strike.

After the strike, the coal companies refused to let replacement workers go and over half the men who went on strike in Lykens Valley were not called back. That didn't help John. But the growth of the anthracite industry did help. The growth of the coal industry, and the Dauphin economy, was jumped-started by the Civil War. John and Adeline's home in Washington Township was only 80 miles from the Mason-Dixon Line and 60 miles from Gettysburg. Thus, Dauphin County, as a breadbasket and coal producer, was important to the Union. Pennsylvania supplied 80 percent of the Union Army's iron, all of its anthracite coal, and much of its textiles and food, with Dauphin a large contributor.

After the Civil War an enormous demand for anthracite and technological advances in mining during the industrial revolution fueled exponential growth in the industry. America's entry into World War I created even more demand. The anthracite industry peaked in 1917, when one hundred eighty thousand workers harvested one hundred million tons of coal throughout the anthracite region of Eastern Pennsylvania. John was one of those workers. He was hired by the Susquehanna Colliery in Lykens in the 1910s. This is evident because in the 1910 census he was a "day laborer" and in 1920 he was a "laborer–coal mine." John was still working for the Susquehanna Colliery in 1922, when a modern electric plant was built to provide electricity to all the local collieries. The $2 million plant burned "coal dirt," or culm, the by-product of coal processing.

John was 67 and still working for Susquehanna in October of 1924, when he was crushed by rolling logs while cutting timber for mine tunnels. He was taken to the Harrisburg Hospital where he died. Cause of death was a hemorrhage and shock from fractured ribs and other injuries. He outlived Adeline by three years. She was fifty-nine when she died of natural causes in 1921. John and Adeline were waked at the Buffington Funeral Home in Elizabethville and buried in St. John's Cemetery.

Though mine work was dangerous and workers were paid less than their value, the pay for a union mine worker in the 1910s and early 20s was better than the average worker's salary in other industries. In the decades before their deaths, John and Adeline may have had some extra income from his job and her farm. Their daughter Beulah, who was ten in 1900, lived with them. As they lived in rural Washington Township they likely had fun taking Beulah to family and church picnics, fairs, moving pictures, and baseball games in the boroughs around the township. They lived on State Road, which was macadam by the 1910s and provided easy access to Elizabethville and Lykens.

In these towns, Adeline could shop at general merchandise and confectionary stores. At the market she could find butter at twenty cents per pound, eggs at eighteen cents per dozen, and dressed chickens at ten cents per pound. As she ran a small farm she may have been a buyer or seller. John might visit taverns, billiard halls, and cigar stores. If they needed to visit the state capital, Harrisburg, twenty miles to the south, they could leave from the train station in Elizabethville—an important troop depot in the Civil War. Built in 1875, the station is still standing today. Also in the towns in the 1880s and 1890s banks were established, rudimentary telephone service began, water companies were organized, and fire departments were formed. Electric lights and moving pictures came in 1909, though these conveniences arrived much later in the townships. They must have seemed like amazing technologies to John and Adeline, who had grown up before electricity, plumbing, and paved roads.

As they traveled among the towns, John and Adeline may have been even more amazed to see a flying machine in the sky. In April of 1913, Walter Johnson of New York flew from Millersburg to Wisconisco in 13 minutes.

Fair going was a pastime. The biggest was seven miles from Lykens in Gratz, which boasted a first-class horse track. At baseball games, John and Adeline might well have watched family members play in the Twin County League. It is known that in 1921, the center fielder, named Wert, set a league record for stolen bases, and a player named Row batted .326 and was third in the league in runs. John and Adeline had at least enough schooling to be literate. Reading newspapers was a popular pastime. The towns all had local papers at one time or another and people also read the Harrisburg Patriot, which chronicled daily life in its town columns. Folks might read that "a coat of paint greatly improved Adam Row's house in Lykens" or "Carrie Wert of Millersburg visited her parents, John, and wife for several days." "Carrie" was a nickname for daughter Caroline.

In addition to his fierce work ethic, John was a devoted family man. In 1920, a grandson, John Schoffer, age seven, lived with him and Adeline. John and Adeline's youngest daughter, Beulah, is the direct ancestor of the Thompson line. After she married James "Edward" Batdorf, they and her parents lived on adjacent farms at 46 and 47 State Road in Washington Township.

See page 136 for photograph of John and Adeline Wert.

JOHN FREDERICK DUNCAN
& CATHERINE MCCLOUD

John Frederick Dankert—later Duncan—was raised in Prussia during the confessional Lutheran migration to the New World, being born April of 1836 in Hohenkirchen, the son of William Gehrhart Heinrich Dankert and Maria Carolina Henriette Kelling of. Frederick was the youngest of six children, living in a time that was extremely difficult for a young man to live with the religious unrest and economic turmoil of that day.

Approximately 5,000 to 7,000 Orthodox Lutherans emigrated to the U.S. for religious reasons over approximately a ten-year span starting in 1839, when the King of Prussia Frederick William III merged the two main religions, Lutheran and Reformed churches.

Crop failure and poor economic conditions were other reasons listed for the mass exodus of Prussia/Germany between 1830 and 1920. Over 700,000 people left the country during that time for America and London.

Possibly spurred on by letters from friends or family who had already emigrated, Frederick made his voyage to the U.S. around the age of 26; most likely entering through New York, where a vast majority of German immigrants entered. The lure of land for as low as $1.25 an acre—due to the Homestead Act of 1862—may have brought him westward to Pennsylvania.

He settled in Sunbury, Pennsylvania, a predominantly Scottish area. As time went by, Frederick's last name was ultimately recorded as Duncan. The change may have been made by the local clerks not knowing how to spell his name or maybe wishing to make a more Anglicized spelling of the Prussian name. Fredrick may have changed his name himself to better fit in with the local population. However, Fredrick kept the latter spelling throughout the rest of his life. All of his children were born with the surname of Duncan.

Sunbury was located near where the north and west branches of the Susquehanna River came together. The town became a port on the Pennsylvania Canal and was a major railroad center. The area boomed with the development of local coalmines and various industries such as textile mills. It is possible that Frederick was working in one of these industries when he met the love of his life, Catherine McCloud. The couple married in 1870.

Catherine McCloud was born and raised in Pennsylvania, as were same as her parents, David McCloud and Mary Zerfass. She lived all of her life in Northumberland County. She was born in Hallowing Run. Eventually her parents, along with their nine children, Joseph, Sarah, Mary Ann, Catherine, Daniel, Frederick, Jeremiah, Judith and William moved to Sunbury the county seat of Northumberland County.

Catherine was 21 when she married Frederick and he was 31. They had six children Melinda, Sarah, William, Gertrude, Hannah Lilly and Charles. They continued to live in Sunbury through their married life.

Sunbury had five dominant religions: Lutheran, Reformed, Baptist, Presbyterian, and Catholic. Fredrick was most likely Lutheran. Catherine may have been Lutheran, but probably converted from one of the other religions when she married Fredrick. Whatever the case may be, all the children were baptized in Zion Evangelical Lutheran Church. Built in 1791, the church is one of the earliest Lutheran churches in America.

In addition to raising their children, both parents worked outside the home. When the couple married, Catherine worked as a housekeeper, possibly at the City Hotel, in Sunbury—where Thomas Edison installed the first successful three-wire electrical lighting system in the U.S. on July 4, 1883.

Sadly they only had twelve years of marriage. Fredrick died in 1882—the same year Charley was born. At the time of his passing, their oldest daughter, Melinda, was only eleven. In the culture of the time, the oldest son would take on the role of the father in this situation, but William was only seven years old at the time of his father's passing.

It must have been very hard for Catherine having so many young children to care for. At the time, there was no welfare system to help a young mother raising six children on her own.

Being the strong and determined woman that she was, Catherine would not take handouts from the neighbors or the church. She sought out employment with higher wages working as domestic help and later as a day laborer, possibly in the textile mills.

Catherine worked hard to support her children before her death in 1903 of dropsy, which today is called edema of the kidney. Her condition was complicated by heart disease. Her legacy of hard work and love undoubtedly held on for generations as the young mother who raised her six children alone and kept her family tightly knit. Most of her children lived out their lives in Sunbury.

Catherine rested knowing that she had raised all of her children to adulthood. Surely one of her last big pleasures was seeing her oldest son, William, marry and carry on the Duncan name. Frederick and Catherine's third child, William, was the direct ancestor of the Thompson line.

JOSEPH PIERCE LAYMAN
& REBECCA JANE OVERLANDER

Just before the outbreak of the American Civil War, on January 8, 1859, Joseph Pierce Layman was born to Michael Layman and Elmira Elizabeth Raymond in Airville, York County, Pennsylvania. He was the seventh of nine siblings: Jacob, Sarah, Uriah, Mary, Elmira, Charles, Lillian, and Theodore.

A short buggy ride away in Chanceford, York County, Pennsylvania, Rebecca Jane Overlander was born in October of the same year to Jacob Warner Oberlander and Sarah Ann Gipe. She was the fifth of eleven siblings: Luther, Sarah, Edward, Adeline, Caroline, Samuel, Margaret, Emaline, Barbara, and Jacob.

Pennsylvanians were strong sympathizers with the Union during the Civil War, sending more than 36,000 men to the battlefields for the North. Joseph's father was one of the many who fought to end slavery and reunite the United States of America. York County sent five companies: Worth Infantry, York Rifles, Marion Rifles, Hanover Infantry, and the York Volunteers to fight for the cause. The 87th Regiment was composed of almost entirely York County men. Joseph's father may have been in one of these regiments.

Joseph and Rebecca may have been too young to understand the full impact of the war, both being very young when the war started. Joseph was aware only that his father was no longer around and may have developed separation anxiety.

They may have been standing along the roadside, wondering what all the commotion was about as their parents and siblings cheered the troops passing through their respective towns. They must have felt the resentment of the Confederate occupation of the City of York in 1863 from their family members. By the time the nearby Battle of Gettysburg and the smaller scrimmages that lead up to it were fought in 1865, they were old enough to feel the ground shake from the cannon explosions and see the hasty movements of troops going to and coming from battle. This must have struck fear and confusion in their young minds.

Nevertheless, they grew up; Joseph probably tending to his parents' dairy cows and crops, which was the main agriculture of the day in most of the rural areas of York County. Airville was a small rural community that had its population counted in the Lower Chanceford census, along with Peach Bottom and Fawn townships.

Rebecca, on the other hand, lived in nearby Chanceford, a larger town where possibly Joseph and his parents sold their milk, butter, and produce. As time went by, Rebecca caught the eye of Joseph, maybe at a town social or dance, or maybe they met when he was delivering his family's products to her mother. We really don't know how they met, but we do know that they were married in 1877 in Chanceford.

Joseph and Rebecca had fourteen children: Lillian, Charlotte "Lottie" (who became the Thompson family matriarch), Earl, Nelson, Charles, Daniel, Chester, Theodore, Joseph, Mabel, Margaret, Ralph, Leroy, and Martha. Shortly after they were married, Joseph and Rebecca moved to Brogueville, York County, Pennsylvania, where Lottie was born. Another move took the family to Columbia, Lancaster County, Pennsylvania possibly for Joseph's job with the railroad. He was a brakeman and then later an engineer. The promotion to engineer could have been the reason the family moved to Sunbury, Northumberland County, Pennsylvania. Rebecca was a homemaker throughout their marriage.

The 1920 census reported Joseph and Rebecca were living in Chicago IL with their youngest children Lee and Martha. Lee was 24 at the time and working as a bookkeeper and Martha was 21 working as a telephone operator. Joseph was 64 and no longer worked for the railroad. 1920 found him working in the storeroom of a packinghouse. Rebecca had no job. Lee is listed as the head of the house. Little is known about why Joseph and Rebecca moved to Chicago. A few scenarios could have played out.

Joseph suffered from valvular heart disease and chronic nephritis and cystitis. The latter is inflammation of the kidneys and bladder. This could have facilitated Joseph and Rebecca to move to Chicago to be closer to specialized medicine of the day. Perhaps Lee and Martha decided to venture out to the big city of Chicago.

With all their children out of the home and Joseph retired, possibly Joseph and Rebecca decided to go along. It could have been Rebecca's health that took the family to Chicago. She passed away in 1921 of Lobar Pneumonia at the Hazelton State Hospital in Pennsylvania. This scenario is unlikely given pneumonia is an acute illness, coming on suddenly, usually when a person's immune system is weak.

A fourth scenario is also possible. During Joseph's many years working as an engineer, he undoubtedly made the run to Chicago many times. This may possibly have been when he met the mysterious Mary, who he married around the time Rebecca was hospitalized in Hazelton. Perchance he may have moved to Chicago to be closer to her and when Rebecca found out about their affair she moved back to Pennsylvania. Grief stricken, Rebecca may have taken ill, which turned into the Lobar Pneumonia that took her life.

We may never know the real reason for the move. Or why Joseph chose not to return to Pennsylvania where most of his children lived. Joseph passed away three years later in 1924 and was buried in Chicago. His cause of death was listed as valvular heart disease and chronic nephritis and cystitis. Joseph and Rebecca's second child, Lottie, was the direct ancestor of the Thompson line.

JAMES M. ANDERSON
& LUCETTA GAUGLER

James Anderson and Lucetta Gaugler were born eight months apart in the village of Chapman, Pennsylvania, which lies on the west bank of the Susquehanna. In the year of their births, 1854, Chapman lay in Union County, but the part of Union County in which they were born would be separated and renamed Snyder County the year after their birth.

Both of their families had deep roots in Union County, Pennsylvania: of their four parents, all but one was born in Union County. That parent, James's mother, Catherine Bordner, had been born in neighboring Northumberland County right across the river.

Born in April of 1854, James was the seventh child of Elijah Anderson and Catherine Bordner Anderson. His older six siblings were Samuel Benjamin, Mary Pamela, Susan, Sarah Adeline, Josephine, and Emma Jane. After James came two sisters, Evaline Edith and Catherine.

Lucetta was born not far away and only eight months later on Christmas Day. She was named after her mother's sister, Aunt Lucetta. Years later, Lucetta's granddaughter Mamie Lucetta Anderson would, in turn, be named after her.

Lucetta's parents were Abraham Gaugler and Kesiah Kelly Gaugler. Like James, she was the seventh child of her family, but her family was even larger, comprised of fifteen children. After bearing a son, a daughter, a son, a daughter, and a son, Kesiah Gaugler went on to give birth to ten daughters in a row. Preceding Lucetta were John, Adeline, George, Emaline, James, and Elizabeth Jane. After Lucetta came Isabelle, daughter K. J., Sarah, Minerva, Alice, Caroline, and Ella.

The birth names of James's and Lucetta's parents suggest that both of them represented the various ethnic strains of early Pennsylvania—its early German population mixed with somewhat later waves of English and Irish immigrants. Anderson is clearly an English name, as Kelly is an Irish name. But both James and Lucetta each also had a parent whose ancestors were part of Pennsylvania's strong German heritage. Bordner, James's mother's maiden name is most likely a variant of the Middle Low German name "Bartner." Gaugler, Lucetta's father's name, stems from South German or Swiss German, with a distant original meaning being "jester" or "entertainer."

In such a small community, the Anderson and Gaugler families were sure to have known each other. James and Lucetta might have been childhood friends. Pennsylvania's 1790 State Constitution had mandated free public primary education. We can well imagine James and Lucetta sitting in the same classroom in a one-room schoolhouse, learning their ABCs and numbers, and walking home together after school.

We can wonder if their childhood friendship gradually blossomed, as they grew older, into friendship, affection, love, and a desire to spend their lives together. Or, did uniting in marriage just seem the logical next step for 19-year-olds whose families had been acquainted for their entire lives?

Marriage in rural America in the 19th century had a somewhat different meaning than it does today. Married couples are expected to care for one another, but in the 19th century the institution of marriage was built upon a religious, legal, and social framework, and marriage was considered to be much more of an economic relationship. With none of the labor-saving devices we take for granted today, division of labor between a man and a woman was essential. It was nearly impossible for a person to live alone.

By the time they were nineteen years old, James and Lucetta had known each other for at least thirteen years. At the very least, their marriage was based on long acquaintance and some degree of affection. Quite possibly, this acquaintance had grown into love. As was typical for married couples of that era, James and Lucetta began a family. Their oldest was Charles, followed in 1880 by William. Then came two more sons, Theodore and Thomas. After four boys in a row, Amy Josephine became the Andersons' first girl. She was joined next by another sister, Catherine.

James and Lucetta continued to reside in Chapman and the adjacent Port Trevorton until James's death in 1899. James was working as a laborer in 1880. There were a number of industries in which a strong, tireless man could find employment. Local mines yielded huge amounts of coal, and laborers were required both at the mines and at the Pennsylvania Canal port that had been dredged in the Susquehanna River at Port Trevorton, giving it the name of "Port."

James might also have worked in the lumber industry, which was still in the process of removing the white pine, Eastern hemlock, and hardwood forests that had once covered 90% of the land area of Pennsylvania.

James might have worked in agriculture, too, since farming was, and still is, an important element of the local economy. In the late 19th century, Snyder County farmers specialized in wheat as a cash crop and corn for livestock feed, dairy cattle, and hogs. In addition, rye was a common crop used in the distilling industry. Other industries that were prominent—and in which James could have worked at one time or another—included tanning, barrel making, gunsmithing, and furniture manufacture.

James could also have worked on Pennsylvania's canal system. In Pennsylvania, a vast network of canals—with locks where necessary—had been dug in order to transport floating logs as well as barges for carrying coal, agricultural products, and passengers. In James's prime working years, some canals were still being dug and they all needed constant maintenance. The total length of Pennsylvania's network of canals eventually exceeded 1,200 miles.

By the year of James's and Lucetta's birth, however, railroads had begun displacing canals, and work for the Pennsylvania Railroad was an important source of employment for residents of Snyder County. James Anderson could have found steady work in any of these industries. Certainly, with a wife and six children, he needed to stay employed.

Though James was the seventh child of his parents, upon his mother Catherine's death in 1893 it fell on him to serve as administrator of probate. Unfortunately, there seems to have been disagreement among the Anderson siblings, with legal documents filed protesting James's administration.

In 1899, at the age of forty-five, James died in Port Trevorton, Pennsylvania. The cause of death was lip and throat cancer. At the end of the 19th century, surgical removal of cancerous tissue was the only available treatment, but it is unlikely that a workingman in rural Pennsylvania would have had access to any kind of surgery. It is likely that his death was prolonged and painful.

Within a year of James's death, Lucetta moved to Sunbury—a larger town about a dozen miles up the Susquehanna River from Port Trevorton. Her oldest son, Charles, was no longer living with his mother, but Lucetta's household still included William, Theodore, Thomas, Amy, and Kate. Life for a widow with five children would have been difficult, but Lucetta could depend upon her older children to work and contribute money to the family's finances. William, the oldest son remaining at home, was employed as a woodworker.

Ten years later, in 1910, Lucetta was left with only one child at home: her daughter Katie. In 1916, at the age of sixty-one, still living in Sunbury, Lucetta passed away as a result of heart disease. She was buried at St. Johns United Methodist Church, Port Trevorton, where her husband James had been buried seventeen years earlier. James and Lucetta's second son, William, born in 1880, was the direct ancestor of the Thompson line.

See page 133 for photographs of James and Lucetta Anderson.

JAMES POLLOCK KEEFER
& EMMA LOUISE LIVEZLY

James Pollock Keefer was born in 1859 in Sunbury, Northumberland County, Pennsylvania. James spent his childhood and teen years living in Sunbury and in the next township to the north, Upper Augusta.

James's parents, Michael A. Keefer and Margaret Matilda Bucher, were life-long residents of Northumberland County. James was raised in a typical 19th-century family, the sixth of seven children. Margaret was James's oldest sibling, followed by Mary, Anna Elizabeth, Alice, and Charles. Then came James followed by his sister Emma J. Keefer.

By the time he was twenty-one, James had briefly moved to Pottsville, about 40 miles to the east in Schuylkill County. In Pottsville, he met Emma Louisa Livezly, who was four years his junior. They were married around 1880, when James was twenty-one and Emma was seventeen.

Emma, the daughter of George Culin Livezly and Anna Maria Kent, was born in Pottsville in November, 1863, and baptized within the month. Emma's birth family was even larger than James's: she was the fifth of eight. George and Anna's first child was John Lawrence. Emma never knew her second brother—George was born in 1857 and died at about one year of age. Then came Emma's two older sisters, Georgeann and Eleanor Loretta. After Emma came George Culin, James, and Annzella.

When James met and married Emma, he was working as a cigar maker in Pottsville. Cigars were almost a necessity for men in those days, and cigar making was a widespread industry including both home manufacture and larger factories. In New York City in 1880, there were more than 1,000 separate cigar-making firms. Tobacco leaf was prepared by workers called "strippers," who carefully removed the heavy stems from the leaves. Then the cigar maker would wrap the leaf in a wrapper, demonstrating the level of his craftsmanship by making a perfectly rolled cigar and minimizing waste. Cigar making was not a pleasant occupation. Tobacco stems and powdered leaves sent thick clouds of dust into the air, and cigar makers spent long hours hunched over their work surfaces.

James and Emma soon moved to Ashland, a small borough twelve miles northwest of Pottsville. Ashland had about 4,000 residents by 1882, the year of

Emma Keefer's birth. Set in an environment of dense forest, in the previous two decades it had become a prominent coal-mining town. It is probable that James relocated the family to Ashland in order to work in the mining industry.

It was in Ashland that their child, Emma Louisa Keefer, given her mother's name certainly as a tribute, was born. Mother Emma died just four days after the birth of their first and only child. Mother Emma was buried in the Pottsville Cemetery in Ashland, Pennsylvania. Emma was confirmed, married, became pregnant, delivered her child and died all within a one year period. She was only eighteen when she passed.

By 1892, James had moved their family to James's hometown, Sunbury. James joined the National Guard serving in the 12th Pennsylvania Regiment, Company E, and worked as a brakeman in the Sunbury railroad yards.

A railroad brakeman was an essential member of a railroad train's crew—he was responsible for applying the brakes to slow the train. Brake levers might be either inside or outside the train cars, and brakemen often had to climb to the top of moving trains to operate the brakes from the roof. In addition, brakemen might be responsible for setting couplings between cars and managing the switches that sent trains from one rail to another. With any of those duties, serious injuries and deaths were not uncommon.

It was in that dangerous occupation that James lost his life. He was only 33, and when he was buried in Penns Sunbury Cemetery and he left behind daughter Emma, Railroading was known as an incredibly dangerous occupation. In fact, seven years after James' death, President Harrison said to Congress, "It is a reproach to our civilization that any class of American workmen should, in the pursuit of a necessary and useful vocation, be subjected to a peril of life and limb as great as that of a soldier in time of war." The Federal Employers Liability Act, which passed in 1908, directly addressed railroads' responsibility for deaths such as James's.

However, in 1892, railroads took no responsibility for the widows and families of workers killed on the job, and daughter Emma was left on her own, eventually relocating to the home of her paternal grandparents Michael and Margaret Keefer, in Sunbury, Pennsylvania. James and Emma's eldest daughter, Emma, was the direct ancestor of the Thompson line.

See page 135 for photographs of James and Emma Keefer.

CHAPTER 6

※

Generation Six

*More precious than our children
are the children of our children.*
—EGYPTIAN PROVERB

Our Sixth Generation includes Alexander and Isabelle Thompson, Michael and Magdalena Goodman, Andrew and Catherine Hensel, Daniel and Sarah Updegrove, Peter and Elizabeth Batdorf, Samuel and Mary Peters, David and Catherine Wert, Daniel & Susan Row, Heinrich and Carolina Dankert, David and Mary McCloud, Michael and Elmira Layman, Jacob and Sallie Oberlander, Elijah and Catherine Anderson, Abraham and Kesiah Gaugler, Michael and Margaret Keefer and George and Anna Livezly, of the early 1880's in Pennsylvania, Louisiana, Scotland and Germany.

ALEXANDER THOMPSON
& ISABELLE STODDART PENMAN

A chill October wind mixed salt air with ash from the smokestacks of Edinburgh and carried it up to the farmlands south of the city as the Thompson family gathered to wait for a seventh child to join the clan. Robert Thompson, born June 1771 in Edgehead, and Janet Russell Thompson, born April 1791 in Borthwick, then married for sixteen years, named the boy Alexander upon his birth on October 22, 1805. Alexander was born in Sauchenside Farm, Cranston, Midlothian, Scotland, and was baptized two weeks later on November third. The older siblings, Christina, Robert, William, Mary, George, and John, ages twelve to one year, quickly took to the new arrival. His sisters, in particular, were expected to help their mother with the younger children. Two younger brothers, John and James, would follow, filling out the family with seven brothers and two sisters.

Edinburgh was growing rapidly in the early nineteenth century, becoming a hub for lawyers and other professionals, and gobbling up nearby land to accommodate its growth. Scottish culture was having its heyday, generating a wealth of philosophy and literature, such as Sir Walter Scott's works of historical fiction. At this time Scotland's capital was known as the "Modern Athens," a place where people of modest birth were afforded the opportunity of rising to wealth and prominence. But the prosperity was not universal, and many poorer Scots sought their fortunes overseas, especially in the growing republic on the far side of the Atlantic.

Alexander Thompson was one of those Scots who found his prospects bleak in his homeland. Despite a quickly growing economy, the population was growing even faster, and competition for work was fierce in 1820s Scotland. As the fifth son in a large family, Alexander could only count on his family to do so much. So he did what many young Scots in his position were doing at the time— he got on a boat headed for America. As was and remains typical of immigrants the world over, Alexander did not take this great journey alone. On the boat with him were his older brother George, George's wife Catherine Penman Thompson, and her younger siblings James, Isabelle, and Robert Penman, aged fifteen, eleven, and two years, respectively. The Nimrod landed in New York on July 9,

1827. Having just come of age at 21 years old, Alexander was excited to get a chance in the "land of opportunity."

That opportunity came after a relatively short westward journey, in Middleport, Pennsylvania, where Alexander found work as a teamster, driving wagons loaded with machinery, timber, and other heavy goods. The Appalachian country northwest of Philadelphia was being developed for its ample natural resources, which were needed for the expanding coastal cities. Over the next few years, Alexander became part of the community in Schuylkill County—home to many other recent immigrants—and he obtained his naturalization papers on July 31, 1834. Having become a citizen and having saved scrupulously, Alexander was ready to put down roots and start a family. He bought some land to farm and set his sights on finding a wife.

He didn't have to look very far, as he had already known the girl who would be his wife for several years at least: his sister-in-law's younger sister, Isabelle Stoddart Penman. Isabelle was born on May 9, 1816, in Newbattle, Scotland, the daughter of David Penman, born December 1775 in Gladsmuir and Elizabeth Stoddart, born about 1780. Isabelle joined an already large family with elder siblings Miriam, John, Margaret, Catherine, Elizabeth, Anne, and James. She was eventually joined by two younger brothers, Alexander and Robert, who were four and eight years younger, respectively.

The Penman family was large and industrious, but they unfortunately lost their father at age 51 in 1826, which likely persuaded Catherine Penman Thompson to take her younger siblings with her from Scotland to America. With only one grown son, getting by with so many mouths to feed would have been difficult, so Catherine was doing her widowed mother a great service in taking some of the younger ones into her care. Eventually, their mother would join them in America, and she ended her days in Pottsville, Schuylkill County, Pennsylvania, in 1849.

When the Thompsons and Penmans set off to America, Isabelle was only eleven years old. However, since their journey, Isabelle had grown into a woman and Alexander had taken notice. The pair had a lot in common, from their nationality to common relatives. Also, Isabelle was the eighth child in a family of ten, circumstances quite similar to Alexander's upbringing. Upon her reaching eighteen years, the two were betrothed. The Thompsons and Penmans celebrated New Year's Day 1835 with a wedding in Pottsville, Schuylkill County,

Pennsylvania. Isabelle wore a dark green dress with a matching cape, suitable to the cold weather, and Alexander sported a brown coat with tails and green vest. The ceremony was held that morning at George and Catherine Thompson's home, and the new marriage was announced at the Presbyterian congregation the following Sunday.

Over the next fifteen years, Isabelle bore ten children. The first four were boys: George, Robert, who died as a child, David, and William. Two girls followed: Elizabeth and Janet; Alexander F. and Robert Bruce came next; and last, Isabelle and James filled out the household. Motherhood was rewarding in many respects for Isabelle, but it was also a risky affair considering the state of medicine at the time. Not long after James' birth, a house that had been full of children's laughter was quieted by the passing of their mother on April 18, 1851, in Pottsville, Schuylkill County, Pennsylvania. She was buried the next day in the York Farm Burial Grounds.

During his years with Isabelle, Alexander worked the land at York Farm in Schuylkill County, and the children grew and learned to work the land as well. While clearing a field on the farm, Alexander discovered veins of anthracite coal. He began selling the coal, which could be easily collected from the surface. Anthracite coal was prized for its high burning temperature and less foul smoke than that produced by bituminous or "soft" coal. Later, this land would become the York Farm Colliery, one of the area's major coal mines.

Following Isabelle's death, the family got an infusion of new energy as Alexander married for a second time. Mary Bast, born in 1833, was not much older than the boys, George being only two years her junior. She was the daughter of Isaac Bast and Catharine Kline. The Bast family had eight children: the eldest son, Benneville; five daughters: Floranda, Rose, Mary, Catharine, and Sarah; and two younger sons: Jacob and Charles.

Despite Mary's youth, she was willing and able to take on the challenge of filling in as mother for Alexander's ten children, ages two to eighteen. What's more, she was also ready to mother her own children. That same year, Mary gave birth to the first of another large brood: a boy she named Isaac in honor of her father. The next year brought George—not to be confused with his half-brother George, the eldest of the family. Continuing the family's penchant to reuse names, the next two daughters were christened Isabelle and Mary. The procreation continued as seven more boys were born: John, Andrew, Charles,

Abraham, Winfield, William, and Elmer. A final daughter was named Rebecca.

The year after Alexander took Mary as his wife, the Thompsons left York Farm and bought a 110-acre farm in Porter Township, a then-undeveloped section of Schuylkill County. Alexander would later sell plots of this land, which would become the town of Sheridan in 1869. Alexander built a gristmill in 1857, then known as Thompson's mill. The mill was later sold to Grimm & Womer, and then to the Reading Company. The 1850s were prosperous for the Thompsons, as the family's property valuation more than doubled during that decade, from $2,000 to more than $5,000. To put that amount in perspective, $5,000 of assets in 1860 calculates to nearly $2 million in the present day.

While Alexander continued the development of his land, the Civil War broke out and three of his sons were called upon to serve in the Union Army. The family's devotion to the Union can also be seen in Alexander's registration as a Republican, and in the names of the younger sons, Abraham L. and William U.S.G., honoring presidents Lincoln and Grant during their terms in office. While those boys were much too young to serve, the older boys, David, William, and Alexander F., enlisted. William Thompson died at Frederick, Maryland, during his service in 1862. The eldest daughter, Elizabeth, also perished during the war while working as a nurse. David and Alexander F. would return intact from the fighting. Alexander F. served for three enlistments, and he would rise to prominence in the community after working his way through law school, becoming a lawyer and state senator.

During the 1860s and 1870s, Alexander continued to expand his business interests. In addition to his farm and mill, around 1860 he took a position as a superintendent overseeing various properties for Potts & Company, which had established the Potts Colliery just over the county line in Columbia County in 1857. Coal companies often owned most, if not all, of the buildings in the new towns that sprung up around their mines, and having a local person of import oversee their properties would have been helpful.

In 1861, Alexander became the owner of a general store. Between 1865 and 1871, he took contract jobs for mines in the area, apparently buying properties and selling them to coal mining companies—in partnership with his father-in-law—as Bast & Thompson. Thus, Alexander Thompson continued to strive with the same earnestness and character that had earned him a place of distinction in his new home until his retirement in 1871.

Having homesteaded twice, married twice, fathered twenty-one children, and started several successful business ventures, Alexander Thompson no doubt inspired a great many of his friends and neighbors. But he, too, was mortal, and his vigor finally left him at the age of 68. He died on December 4, 1873, in Tower City, Schuylkill County, Pennsylvania, and was laid to rest in Greenwood Cemetery underneath an impressive monument. His son Charles would join him there in 1878. His wife Mary, his junior by 28 years, lived a long life and was finally laid to rest with her husband in 1910 at the age of 76. Alexander Thompson's legacy would continue well beyond his lifespan, shaping the community through his multitudinous progeny and the various commercial interests he had a hand in starting. His son Robert Bruce Thompson was a direct ancestor of the Thompson family line.

MICHAEL GOODMAN
& MARY MAGDALENA BROWN

On a hot summer day, near the steaming banks of the Susquehanna River, John George Gutman and his wife, Susan Brown, welcomed a son. Michael Goodman, born on June 10, 1806, in Lower Mahanoy, Northumberland County, Pennsylvania, was the youngest of four, having elder brothers, Benjamin and Daniel, and a sister. At the age of two, perhaps in anticipation of coming hard times and the death of his father, Michael was taken to live with his grandfather in Berks County, Pennsylvania. The Goodman children would soon be sorrowed by the loss of their mother, Susan, a few years later.

Michael stayed with his grandfather until he was eighteen, when he moved to a farm south of Clarks Valley Road in Dauphin County, Pennsylvania, where he would live out his days. In the next year or so, he was confirmed in the Lutheran congregation at the old log church-school in Schuylkill County, Pennsylvania.

At the age of twenty-four, Michael married Mary Barbara Ramp, who was born about 1805. The couple would bear six children between 1835 and 1846. William, the eldest, would take over the farm and care for his father in his old age. William was followed by two sisters, Susan and Magdalena, then a brother, John. Two more girls, Sarah, known as Sallie; and Catherine, were the last children from this union.

In the 1830s and 1840s, Pennsylvania was the young republic's bread basket. With a climate similar to much of Europe, settlers were able to bring the bulk of their farming knowledge to use in this region, growing fruits and grains from Europe, as well as adopting native plants and techniques. Pennsylvania farmers produced grains, meats, and dairy products, as well as manufactured products such as leather and flaxseed oil. In 1840, more than 77 percent of the 4.8 million employed persons in Pennsylvania were occupied in agriculture.

Mary Barbara unfortunately passed in 1846, likely due to complications from Catherine's birth. After some fifteen years of marriage, Michael—being in his early forties—was now a very eligible widower with many good years left in him. Soon the area matchmakers set to work finding a wife to once again make the farmstead a home.

A woman from the area—who was also older than the usual marrying age—proved to be a suitable match. Mary Magdalena Brown, daughter of Peter Brown and Anna Maria Carl, was a decade Michael's junior, being born in 1816 in Rush, Dauphin County, Pennsylvania. Following the custom that her family had brought from Europe, she went by Magdalena. She was the fifth of eight children, having elder siblings John, Peter, William, and Anna. Her younger siblings were Philip, Rebecca, and Elizabeth. They were grandchildren to Peter Braun, who fought for the British during the Revolution and, interestingly after the War, secured a job working for George Washington. Michael Goodman and Magdalena Brown were married about 1848 in Schuylkill County, Pennsylvania.

Michael and Magdalena had four children. Anna was born later in the same year they were married and two boys, Jacob and George, were to follow. Amid the joys of a new set of births, another tragedy befell the family as Catherine, the youngest child from Michael's first marriage, passed away about 1855, only about nine years old. The family was completed with the birth of Lydia, the last child, in 1856.

During this period, Michael took to working as a carpenter. Since by the 1850s his older sons were teenagers and thus able to take over a large part of the farm work, the head of the household was free to pursue a new craft. Between farming and carpentry, the Goodman family did well in the tumultuous years from 1850 to 1870, increasing their net worth from $1,000 to more than $2,200—more than $600,000 in modern equivalents.

The Goodman farm endured changing times and adapted accordingly. In the middle of the century, railroads were spreading into new regions of the rapidly expanding nation. The railroads brought access to the vast prairies of the Midwest and the Great Plains, and to ever-increasing supplies of grains and meat. The farmers of the east had to adapt to these changing markets. Wheat production was being replaced with milk, butter, hay, potatoes, poultry, eggs, and other products that were needed in the fast-growing urban populations of Philadelphia and Baltimore. This period also saw the early stages of mechanization on farms, as binders and harvesters changed the Northern farm economy and the cotton gin revolutionized the South.

These changes contributed to the growing rift between the regions, eventually exploding into the Civil War. It is likely that John, the second son, enlisted in 1861 at the age of twenty. John was fortunate to return home, marry, and have a family. It appears that this branch of the Goodman family was not fated to grieve for a lost son, as many of their neighbors and relatives were.

After many prosperous years, the 1880s brought the ravages of age to the Goodman family. Michael and Magdalena had enjoyed 36 years together, but again Michael found himself outliving a wife. At the age of 68, Magdalena died on December 17, 1884 in Tower City, Schuylkill, Pennsylvania. She was laid to rest at Zion Public Square Lutheran Cemetery, Tower City, Schuylkill County, Pennsylvania. Michael would not be alone after his second wife's passing; he spent his golden years living on the farm—which had become his son William's livelihood—surrounded by his many children and grandchildren.

In what would be his final summer, Michael Goodman hosted a great gathering of his family on Sunday, August 19, at the farmstead. "The family dinner was spread in bountiful manner under the ancient cherry tree, and a happy feast was enjoyed by all present, numbering 43 persons of the Goodman freundschaft. At the planting of that cherry tree, great grandfather Michael Goodman, who was 94 years of age in June, did not think of such a gathering under its branches, and as the venerable father offered thanks at the dinner table, he expressed the desire that they would all meet at the festal board of Heaven."

Clearly Michael was anticipating the inevitable: he died on December 27, 1900, in Rush, Dauphin County, Pennsylvania. The West Schuylkill Herald recorded his passing: "Michael Goodman, the oldest and best-known citizen of this valley, died at the home of his son, William, in Clarks Valley at three a.m. last Thursday morning. His death was due to old age. . . . The deceased was probably the oldest man in the valley, being 94 years, 6 months, and 17 days. He followed farming for a living and retained great vitality up until about a year ago. Up to that time he frequently walked from his home to Williamstown, a distance of four miles. For the past year, however, his health had been failing. He was only bedfast, however, a short time before death overtook him. Early in his life he connected with the Evangelical Church. When the split occurred, he chose the United Evangelical. It is said that for 72 years he was a member and took great delight in church work. The funeral was held Sunday morning. Services were conducted in the U E Church by the pastor, Reverend S N Dissinger, assisted by Reverend C E Hess of Williamstown. Interment was made in the cemetery in this place." Michael Goodman rests in Zion Public Square Lutheran Cemetery, Tower City, Schuylkill County, Pennsylvania.

The Evangelical Church, a predecessor to the modern United Methodist Church, suffered a division in 1894. Nearly a third of the denomination split off and formed the United Evangelical Church, while the remainder was known as the Evangelical Association. United Evangelical members were generally more progressive, favoring the use of English language rather than the traditional German, greater local control, and less authoritarian leadership. The schism was largely about personalities and culture rather than about theology, but it was serious nonetheless. "In some congregations, the controversy divided families, led to verbal and physical attacks, and ended in court battles over the church property. Eventually, or as some have said, 'when enough funerals had taken place,' the factions reunited in 1922 to form the Evangelical Church." Since the secular courts sided with the Evangelical Association regarding ownership of church property, many United Evangelical congregations were starting from the ground up in the 1890's, and thus Michael's leadership in his congregation was likely needed and much appreciated. *The Tower City, Porter Township Centennial* writes:

Michael Goodman was born June 10, 1806, and came to this valley as a young man and was confirmed in the old log church-school in July 1825, according to the old church records. He married Mary Magdalena Brown, a granddaughter of the original Peter Braun. Michael purchased the farm south of the Clark's Valley Road just east of the Dauphin County line and lived there until his death on December 27, 1900, at the grand age of ninety-four. His wife died December 17, 1884, and both are buried in the cemetery in the public square. In his later years, he gave his farm to his son William, who was born November 20, 1835, and died January 30, 1907. He married Christina Hand, a daughter of John Hand, Jr., and they had the following children: Catherine, who first married Lincoln Rhoads and on his death married Herman Niehenke; Ernaline, who married Elwood Showers; Mary, wife of Isaac Thompson; John; Lydia, married Nathan A. Reightler; George; Fayetta, married William Achenbach; Frank; Ellen, wife of William Novinger; and David. John Goodman married Hannah Houtz and their children were Harry II, Charles E., Golda, and Grace. Harry married Sadie P. Warfield and their child was Helen; Evelyn, married Frank Rosade; Lillian P.; John; Stuart; and Virginia, married J. Robert Hunsicker. Among the children of Ernaline Goodman Showers and her husband were Albert; Charles; Roy; Beulah, married George Schrope; Verna, married Robert Fegley. The children of

Charles Showers were Lester; Helen; Anne, married Norman Unger; Violet; and Lawrence. A very pleasant and enjoyable affair was the reunion of the Goodman family, on Sunday, August 19, at the residence of Mr. and Mrs. William Goodman, in Clarks Valley, which is also the birthplace of Mr. Goodman. The following were present: Mrs. Isaac Thompson and children, Paul, Russel and Leona, Sheridan; Mr. and Mrs. Elwood Showers and children, Charles, Beulah, Raymond, Emma, Verna, and Albert, Tower City; Mr. and Mrs. David Goodman and children, Clarence and Elva, Orwin; Mrs. John Goodman and children, Harry, Charles, and Golda, Orwin; Mrs. Wm. Achenbach and children, Harry, Roy, and Frank of Philadelphia; Mrs. Catherine Rhoads and children, Charles, Oscar, Ira, Millie, and Lloyd, Sheridan; Mr. and Mrs. Nathan Rightler and children, Emily and Willie, Tower City; Frank Goodman and son George, Orwin; George Goodman, Clarks Valley; Mr. and Mrs. Wm. Novinger and daughter, Hattie; Tower City. Artist Rowland of Williamstown photographed the group under an old cherry tree planted scores of years ago by great grandfather Michael Goodman, who was also in attendance. The family dinner was spread in bountiful manner under the ancient cherry tree, and a happy feast was enjoyed by all present, numbering 43 persons. At the planting of that cherry tree, great grandfather Michael Goodman, who was 94 years of age in June, did not think of such a gathering under its branches, and as the venerable father offered thanks at the dinner table, he expressed the desire that they would all meet at the festal board of Heaven. May his desires be granted. As the hour arrived for the happy parties to return to their respective homes, all seemed to realize that in the changing scenes of time, another such a gathering might never occur in this world. After 60 years of earthly pilgrimage, Mr. and Mrs. Wm. Goodman were favored by a kind providence in the gathering of all their sons and daughters, with thirty of the grandchildren. It was an occasion of great joy of retrospective glances over the journey of life, and happy anticipations of a reunion in the golden world of eternal deliverance.

> *During that gathering, a poet expressed:*
> *Scattered o'er various fields by Heaven,*
> *Through various pathways led,*
> *What happiness in peace to meet*
> *Around a common head!*

The pleasures of the past recall,
And tell the tales again
Its infant dreams, and childhood joys,
And youth's delightful reign,
To plan the schemes of future bliss;
Rejoicing to confess,
That He whose love hath blessed the past
The future, too, will bless.

Michael Goodman's youngest daughter, Lydia Ann Goodman, would marry Robert Bruce Thompson, and their progeny would carry the Thompson name to the present generation.

ANDREW G. HENSEL & MARY A. GUISE

Andrew Guise Hensel was born on February 18, 1831, at home in New Bloom-field, Perry County, Pennsylvania. New Bloomfield is in the central Pennsylvania countryside, west of the Susquehanna River, an area then being rapidly developed for farming and industry. Named after his father, Andrew was the fifth of six children, preceded by his brother John Adam, sister Anna, and brothers John and George. After Andrew came Michael Hensel, who would later become a reverend. Andrew's father was Andrew W. Hensel, a shoemaker, born in Littlestown, near Gettysburg, Adams County, Pennsylvania, and his mother was Mary Guise, born in Northampton County, Pennsylvania.

The Hensel family had been shaped by significant military experience. Andrew W. Hensel served in the War of 1812 as a private. He was among the noncommissioned officers and privates from Captain John McMillan's company, Colonel Fenton's regiment, of the Pennsylvania Militia, who crossed the Niagara into Canada, and also served in Buffalo, New York. The Hensels' military pedigree extended another generation back as well. Both of Andrew's grandfathers, John Casper Hensel and John Adam Guise, served in the American Revolution, in York County, Pennsylvania, under Captain Will, and in Northampton County, Pennsylvania, under Captain Drapper, respectively.

When Andrew went to work, he garnered early experience as a servant, but he soon took up the profession of plasterer, playing a part in the spread of housing that came along with the ongoing expansion of mining in Pennsylvania. The steady influx of miners to the region generated demand in his field, so Andrew was able to enjoy a stable income and confidence in his plans to start a family.

At twenty-two years of age, Andrew would marry Anna Catherine Workman—known as Catherine—on March 17, 1853, amid St. Patrick's Day festivities in Halifax, Dauphin County, Pennsylvania. Never mind that they were married in a Methodist Episcopal congregation. Since most of the early immigrants to America from Ireland were Protestants, the holiday had not yet taken on the Catholic associations that became common in the late 1800s into the twentieth century. Rather, the Americans of the young republic celebrated St. Patrick's Day primarily as an act of anti-colonial solidarity with the Irish in their struggle for freedom from English rule. Since the two families were situated close to one another, it was likely a well-attended wedding, filling the building with friends and relatives on a Thursday morning as the beginnings of spring were just becoming noticeable in the hilly Pennsylvania countryside.

Catherine, the daughter of Joseph Workman and Susan Romberger, was born in Old Lincoln, Dauphin County, Pennsylvania, on May 17, 1838. She was only fourteen years old on her wedding day. Since she was the youngest of nine children, it is likely that economic concerns contributed to her early marriage. This was a common fact of life for the families of the working class at the time. Her sisters, Susan, Nancy, Elizabeth, and Carolina, reassured and advised the girl as the wedding approached and throughout the marriage. Catherine had helped her sisters with their children, so she was aware of the duties and troubles of raising children. And she also knew something of the joy that children brought to a home. Of course, her four older brothers, Jacob, John, Henry, and Joseph, were surely protective of their youngest sister, but the repute of the Hensel family—and the two families' shared military history—may have eased any concerns about the match. Joseph, Catherine's father, served in the War of 1812, and her grandfather Balthasar Romberger and great-grandfather Jacob Lehman both served in the American Revolution in Lancaster County, Pennsylvania.

Soon the Hensel family was growing. Their first son, John, was born in the year they married, but he did not survive infancy. Catherine's pain eased slowly as more sons came quickly. The next year brought Joseph, then Ira two years later, and Howard after another two years. The family's growth slowed as the Civil War broke out and Andrew left home to serve in the Union Army.

In September 1862, Andrew Guise Hensel was mustered into Company F of the 155th Regiment of the Pennsylvania Infantry at Harrisburg. This unit would be attached to the 2nd Brigade, 3rd Division, 5th Army Corps, Army of the Potomac immediately after reaching Washington, where they were held in reserve during the battle of Antietam. Though they did not fight, the soldiers suffered the elements in these early days of the war due to a lack of basic provisions such as tents and uniforms. A great deal of these needs eventually were donated to units in the Army of the Potomac from the soldiers' communities back home. The 155th first fought at the battle of Fredericksburg that December, during which they suffered heavy losses in an unsuccessful series of charges. "Captain Lee Anshultz was mortally wounded, dying the following day, and the color-sergeant, and the entire color guard were shot down." They also witnessed defeat near Chancellorsville, holding defensive positions. The 155th was later assigned to the 2nd Brigade, 2nd Division of the 5th Corps. At the battle of Gettysburg, the 155th was instrumental in the taking of Little Round Top on the second day of fighting, which helped secure the Union Army's defenses. They held that position on the following day, witnessing the final rebel charge from their unchallenged defensive position, and later pursued the retreating enemy.

The battle at Gettysburg helped to shape the unit's identity and likely contributed to the wealth of documentation available on the subject. A succession of injuries leading to honorable discharges among the officers in the wake of that battle led to the promotion of Alfred L. Pearson to Colonel. Pearson and other officers of the 2nd Brigade led these men in learning the tactics of the French Light Infantry and adopted variations of French-style uniforms to match their inspiration. They came to be known as the Zouave Brigade, which included several units of infantry from Pennsylvania and New York, however the trend was more widespread. Units from nearly all of the states on both sides—and the District of Columbia—styled themselves as Zouaves. The Zouaves of the 155th wore a light blue jacket with yellow trimming and tombeaus, or stylized false pockets; baggy blue trousers; and a red sash with matching red fez. They certainly drew a stark contrast with the straight lines and dark blue of the typical Union Army uniform. Subsequently, the unit was attached to various other brigades up until May 1864, when the unit would be reorganized as the 191st Regiment of the Pennsylvania Infantry. Private Hensel was assigned to Company G.

Pearson's Zouaves fought in many other battles and suffered great hardship: in one battle having 83 men killed or wounded in just ten minutes. But they also saw success, and Pearson was promoted to Major General before the war had ended, which happened before their eyes as the white flag was raised just as the Zouaves were heading into the town of Appomattox Court House for another fight.

Victory meant an end to the bitter suffering this unit had witnessed. Over two years and nine months of service, the combined losses for the 155th and 191st Regiments were six officers, 248 enlisted men killed or mortally wounded, and 272 enlisted men lost to disease—not to mention the death and destruction suffered by Confederates and civilians as well. The unit was mustered out at

Washington on June 2, 1865, and then welcomed home with a celebration in Pittsburgh, as many of the men had been recruited from that region.

The war years were terrible, but also wondrous for Andrew Hensel as his wife, Catherine, gave him four daughters between 1862 and 1866: Anna Catherine (named after her mother), Lillian, Anna, and Emma. In the postwar years, the sons of the Hensel family went to work in various professions, and continued expansion in the mining industry fueled Andrew's career as a plasterer. Wages in his field appear to have been good enough to raise a large family, though Andrew never accumulated a great deal of wealth.

The bustling Hensel household fell silent in grief as the children lost their mother to untimely death at only 38 years old. Anna Catherine Workman died on February 10, 1877, in Joliett, Schuylkill County, Pennsylvania. She was laid to rest in Calvary United Methodist, Wiconisco, Dauphin County, Pennsylvania. The daughters were still living at home, though at fifteen Lillie was capable of taking on many of her mother's household responsibilities. Howard, the youngest son—then eighteen years old—continued to live at home at least until 1880, working as a laborer to support the younger children.

Eventually Andrew found himself ready to move forward after losing his wife of nearly 24 years. The family would have a stepmother when Andrew married Grace Arrison, though this union produced no children.

In the coming years, Andrew took to working as a mason and also as a school teacher. At the turn of the century, he was living as a boarder, likely exchanging his knowledge and experience for room and board. In 1908, Andrew got ill, diagnosed with Bright's disease, a chronic inflammation of the kidneys. After a sickness of a few months he died at age 77 on December 14, 1908, in Wiconisco, Dauphin County, Pennsylvania. Two days later he was put to rest in Calvary United Methodist Cemetery, Wiconisco, Dauphin County, Pennsylvania. His headstone was adorned with a flag-holder star marked G.A.R. for the Grand Army of the Republic, honoring his service in the Union Army.

A veteran, a father of eight children and grandfather of many, Andrew Guise Hensel lived through great upheavals and the steady pressure of America's industrial development. Andrew's son Howard Andrew Carson Hensel was the direct ancestor of the Thompson line.

DANIEL UPDEGROVE & SARAH A. CULP

Life was hard in the anthracite coal fields of eastern Pennsylvania following the Panic of 1837. Layoffs, wage cuts, and persistently high unemployment afflicted the nation, dooming President Van Buren's re-election campaign. John M. Updegrove, a laborer from Berks County, Pennsylvania—the son of Conrad Updegrove and Maria Elizabeth Angst—and his wife, Elizabeth Reisch—the daughter of Frederick Reisch and Veronica Schmidt—were struggling to keep their growing family fed. The couple had been married for fourteen years when they welcomed their fifth child, Daniel, on June 28, 1839. His siblings Jacob, Catherine, John, and Nancy were excited, but his parents' joy was tempered with worry. By that time, eldest Jacob was old enough to be allowed to work. Though still a child, this would only be a help if there were work to be had. Two more children, Solomon and Rebecca, would come along in the middle of the next decade.

The Updegrove children were afforded basic education, but like most children of the day they also went to work at a young age. As a young man, Daniel became a blacksmith's apprentice, but within a few years he started working as a coal miner. In the 1860s, the coal country of Pennsylvania was in full production, continuously expanding the mines and fueling the Union's war effort.

During the early days of the war, Daniel met and soon married Salome A. Culp, a girl five years his junior, born June 30, 1844, in Union County, Pennsylvania. Her parents, Jacob Culp and Elizabeth Schneck, had one son and five daughters. Salome—commonly called Sarah—and her siblings lost their mother in 1861, while Daniel and Salome were courting. Jacob found his house emptying quickly, but still he was pleased to see his second youngest married at the age of eighteen. The eldest brother, Jonas, who was Daniel's age, respected Daniel and trusted him to care for his little sister. Elizabeth, Henrietta, and Esther advised their younger sibling about her coming role as a wife, and fourteen-year-old Fielta seemed quite taken with Mr. Updegrove. The handsome young man with sandy hair and grey eyes had actually charmed the entire family. On October 9, 1862, there was a wedding at the Culp house, attended by neighbors, friends, and family. The young couple would not have an easy start in their new life, however, as Daniel would soon be enlisted in the war effort.

Inspired by tales of his great-grandfather John Daniel Angst, who volunteered in Berks County and served under Captain Bretz in the American Revolution, several members of the Updegrove family would fight in the war, including Aaron Updegrove, Daniel Updegrove, Henry K. Updegrove, John Updegrove, and Solomon Updegrove.

Daniel and his brother Solomon signed up in July 1863 to fight for the Union. Enlisting in Harrisburg, the two were placed under Captain Edward Savage as privates in the 9th Cavalry, Company B, of the 92nd Regiment Pennsylvania Volunteers. This unit was known as the Lochiel Cavalry. This distinctively named unit's exploits were quite well known even during the war through the regular correspondence of Private George Unkle with the Daily Evening Express. The unit saw extensive action in Kentucky and Tennessee, facing off against Confederate cavalry units that had given the Union army trouble in the early phases of the war. Accounts of the Lochiel Cavalry paint a heroic picture of determined men crossing rugged terrain "on half rations, food half cooked, and boots worn off their feet by tramping over the rocks to ease their own good horses, and trusting to Providence to keep down the wide and swift rivers that drain these wild mountains," as they set to destroy key railways and outmaneuver foes.

Standing 5 foot 5 inches, Private Daniel was built well for riding, light enough that his horse would not wear out too quickly. The Updegrove brothers served with honor, surviving many battles. Solomon was struck down in action at Waynesboro, Georgia, on December 4, 1864. This loss pained Daniel for the rest of his days. As a particularly strange coincidence, another Pennsylvania man, Solomon S. Updegrove, who served in the 18th Cavalry, 163rd Regiment, survived the war and went on to become a prominent citizen. This peculiarity likely added to Daniel's grief over his dead brother.

But the war was not yet over, and Daniel's suffering was not quite through. Not long after losing his brother, Daniel was captured and held as a prisoner of war for twenty-one days in Libby Prison, at Richmond, Virginia. This aged warehouse on the banks of the James River caused the death of many Union soldiers due to illness, exposure, and starvation. The windows were barred but not shut, and the prison was so overcrowded that men covered every bit of floor as they attempted to sleep through their shivering. While some died quickly, others endured for months, even digging an underground tunnel and staging a successful escape. In the largest prison escape of the war, 109 Union POWs made their way single-file through the tunnel. Discovery of the escape was delayed until morning, helping 59 of the inmates to escape safely under the command of Captain Tower and Colonel Davis. Two men drowned in the James River, and 48 were recaptured. Daniel was lucky to only stay there for three weeks before being released, likely when the Union Army overtook Richmond on April 3, 1865. On that day much of the city burned as Confederates attempted to destroy stockpiled goods and the nearly starved populace of the city rioted.

Despite the suffering and uncertainty of the war, Daniel was able to make it home to his wife on occasion. They welcomed a daughter, Anna, in 1864. Another daughter, Clara Matilda, came two years later, followed by William Henry, who died as an infant in 1871, and Nora Jane, born in 1874. With only three surviving children, the Updegrove household was not large for the time, but it was full of activity. Daniel returned to mining after the war and the family subsisted on this moderate livelihood. In 1870, the family claimed $100 in property.

Both Daniel and Sarah had only a few years of schooling, having been pulled away from school to work in their youth. The 1870 census shows that they were able to read but not able to write. However, either through private study or community effort, by the next census the pair were deemed literate. Perhaps the intermittent unemployment due to accidents, labor disputes, and disruptions in the market that was characteristic of a coal miner's life—he had been unemployed for four months in 1880—afforded Daniel sufficient time for self-education.

Hard luck characterized much of Daniel's professional life. In 1887, Daniel lost a lawsuit over some 50 acres of property possessed by Mr. J. M. Blum—upon which much of the town of Williamstown was built—that had been previously owned by Daniel's father, John. John Updegrove had filed the same claim and lost in 1875, and Daniel was bringing the claim up again following his father's death. Residents of Williamstown were not overly worried, counting the case as a long shot, and indeed Updegrove's case was soon dismissed by the Pennsylvania Supreme Court. At 48 years old, Daniel's prospects for advancement were not bright. He had lost the case and there was little for him to do but continue as a miner.

The Brookside Colliery was one of the most productive coal mines in the world through much of the nineteenth century and into the twentieth century. It was under continual expansion at the tail end of the 1800s, with new slopes being sunk. One of the great challenges of engineering the expansion of mines was providing adequate ventilation. As the mine is expanded, the amount of airflow required to prevent coal dust from accumulating and igniting also increases. This expensive and time-consuming work was a bane of contention between management and labor, as demands for profits versus a safe working environment fueled labor activism. This antagonistic relationship was often rekindled when such an accident would occur. One such tragedy came on May 23, 1899, claiming the life of Daniel Updegrove, who was suffocated by mine gas likely caused by an explosion. He was laid to rest a few days later, on May 28, just short of 60 years old, in Seyberts Lutheran Cemetery in Williamstown, Dauphin County, Pennsylvania.

Daniel would be survived by his wife, Sarah, and their three daughters. Daniel's military pension was a help to the family, but Sarah ended up taking work as a domestic servant to make ends meet. Salome would live to watch the family grow and to help them carry on through hard times, including the growing pains of mechanization in the mines and the similarly mechanized Great War in Europe. Eventually, a recurrent case of carcinoma of the shoulder would bring her to rest at the age of 79. She was reunited with her husband on July 6, 1923, in Seyberts Lutheran Cemetery.

Daniel and Sarah's descendants would proliferate in the new century, their daughter Clara Matilda being the direct ancestor of the Thompson line.

PETER BATDORF & ELIZABETH WELKER

In a sense, Peter Batdorf and his wife, Elizabeth Welker, were war babies. She was born on November 23 in 1812, four months after America declared war on Great Britain beginning the War of 1812. He was born January 20, 1814, eleven months before the treaty was signed ending the war. The war must have seemed distant to their families—the only Pennsylvania battle was at Lake Erie. News of the battle probably took a month to reach Dauphin County, Pennsylvania.

Peter and Elizabeth were born in Lykens Township, Dauphin County, at a time when America was less than forty years old. She was named for her mother, Maria "Elizabeth" Messerschmidt, he for his father, Jacob "Peter" Batdorf. Lykens is named for Andrew Lycans, as it was commonly spelled at the time. He settled on a tract of about two hundred acres on the Whiconescong Creek in 1755, near what is now Loyalton Borough. He cleared land and built houses for his family and a small group of subsequent settlers. Lycans lived in relative peace for no more than a year.

Then in 1756, during the French and Indian War, Lycans was driven from his home and eventually died while retreating from Indians. The Indians were allied with the French against the British and the colonists. The hostilities with the Indians ended in 1764, after which Lycan's widow returned to the old home.

By 1810, when Peter was born, the Indians had been driven to the west. Peter was the first of nine children of Jacob Peter Batdorf and Maria Catherine Steiner. Sarah, John, Catherine, Thomas, Jonathan, Daniel, Jacob, and Elizabeth were Peter's young siblings. Peter's father, Jacob, was born in 1793. His mother, Maria, was born in 1792. Though it's not known if Jacob was born in Dauphin County, it is certain that he lived and died there. Maria was born in adjacent Berks County. How she migrated to the Lykens area of Dauphin County isn't clear. It may have been with her family or after she married Jacob. In either case, it may have been no more than ten to fifteen miles.

Elizabeth Welker was the fourth child of John Welker and Maria Elizabeth Messerschmidt, both natives of Dauphin County. John was born in 1783, Maria Elizabeth in 1780. Elizabeth followed siblings George, Rachel, and a daughter whose name is not known. Her younger siblings were William, David, Anna, Sarah, and Joseph.

Peter was nineteen and Elizabeth was twenty-one when they were married in 1831, most likely in St. Peter's Reformed Church in nearby Loyalton. Also known as the Hoffman Church, it was erected about 1771 by Anthony Hautzon on land donated by the Hoffman family, early settlers in Lykens Township. Peter was baptized there and both he and Elizabeth were buried there. They both died in Dauphin County—she in 1868, he in 1880.

In each census during their lifetimes, Peter and Elizabeth were counted in Lykens Township—not to be confused with Lykens Borough, which was settled within the township in 1832, but not incorporated until 1871. The township was incorporated in 1810 covering fifty square miles in northern Dauphin County. In 1839, it was divided to form Wisconisco Township. In the pre-Civil War nineteenth century, Lykens Township was a remote area of scattered farms in a stunning green valley teeming with wildlife and fishing creeks. The population density was less ten per square mile.

Peter and Elizabeth would live out their lives where they were born. It's not likely they ever traveled more than ten to twenty miles from their home. There was nothing unusual about that. Travel was by wagon over dirt roads that were little more than widened and packed Indian trails. Moving a large family would have been daunting. Besides where would Peter and Elizabeth go, and to do what?

The American economy took off after the War of 1812. The steam engine, patented in 1783 by James Watt, came into widespread use in factories and mills, especially in New England and major cities in the East. But the Industrial Revolution was slow in coming to remote and sparsely populated rural areas like the Lykens Valley. There were no factories in the Dauphin County in the early decades of the nineteenth century. The first known stationary steam engine, as opposed to those used in trains and the ferries at Millersburg and Harrisburg, was brought to Lykens in 1830, when the Lycans settlement consisted of no more than thirty log homes.

Because of these conditions, the Lykens Valley economy was only marginally monetary-based before the Civil War. Self-sufficiency and barter drove the citizens' lives. Peter was self-sufficient as a Yeoman. Though "Yeoman" is commonly thought of as a low naval rank in nineteenth-century America, it also meant a family farmer who owned a small plot of land. Elizabeth kept house and probably made clothes to be handed down for their eleven children, at least in the early years of their marriage. While the first store was opened in the Lykens settlement in 1832, it wasn't until after the Civil War that mercantiles offered factory-made clothes affordable to average folks like the Batdorfs.

Esther was the first born of Peter and Elizabeth's children, followed by Jonas, Elizabeth, Susan, John, Sarah, Peter, Anna, Rebecca, Thomas, and Louisa. The family was closer to average than large for the time period.

Peter was probably a Yeoman for the first a decade or so of their marriage. In the 1840s, as Dauphin became more connected by canals and rail, he may have farmed cash crops such as wheat. In 1825, coal was discovered on Short Mountain overlooking Lykens Valley. This was no ordinary coal, but anthracite of the first order—89 percent carbon. It was shipped crudely by wagon until 1832, when the Lykens Valley Railroad and Coal Company was created by an act of the legislature. The railroad created a need for coal mining laborers that grew exponentially when local breakers were built, the first in Dauphin County in 1848 in Lykens.

Steam engines would come into widespread use in Dauphin with the rise of the coal industry. They were used to drive pumps, fans and conveyers before the collieries made electricity. The breakers increased coal production for the Civil War effort, the growth of factories, and large-scale iron forges. The need for laborers could be met only one way—immigration. They came from Scotland, Ireland, Germany, and other parts of Europe, doubling the population of Dauphin County in the mid-nineteenth century. Though the anthracite mines were notorious for accidents and worker exploitation, the coal greatly enhanced the Dauphin economy and sped technological advances.

Peter entered his fifties during the Civil War. He was too old to be drafted, but took advantage of the ancillary jobs created by burgeoning coal industry and the war. Peter worked as a carpenter from 1850 to 1870. He may have been building log homes and churches for immigrant families. He might also have helped build furniture, canal locks, or railroads ties.

After Elizabeth died in 1868, Peter married Magdalena "Mollie" Lettich. His marriage to Mollie, and his advancing age, may have prompted Peter to go back to farming. He may have been aided by organizations of farmers, such as the Grange, that fought to improve the conditions for yeomen. The Pennsylvania Grange was organized in 1873.

When Peter and Mollie married they were beyond childbearing years, but Peter and Elizabeth's second youngest, Thomas, was the direct ancestor of the Thompson line.

SAMUEL PETERS & MARY LOUISE SWARTZ

How remote was Union County, Pennsylvania, when Samuel Peters was born there in 1821? In 1821, the Pennsylvania Canal system hadn't yet reached Union. A railroad connection was forty-plus years away. Fewer than fifty years earlier, the area was on the frontier of European settlement.1 The County had been formed in 1813 when land west of the Susquehanna River was separated from Northumberland County. It was divided into Union and Snyder counties in 1855. Samuel was the first born of five children of John and Anna Maria Peters. Anna's maiden name is unknown. Samuel was followed by brothers, Andrew, Jonathan, Elias, and a sister, Matilda.

Samuel's father, John, was born in New Jersey in 1795 and migrated to Union County, Pennsylvania where he met and married Anna. It is very likely he migrated just a year or so before Samuel was born in 1821 and settled in Buffalo Township. As with most of the early settlers of Union County, John likely migrated there for work or to acquire land, which was being allotted by application.

When Samuel grew up he did not go to school, as there weren't any in the Buffalo area. In 1834, the state legislature passed a bill mandating counties to create common, or public, schools. Afraid of the cost, most of which had to be met at the local level, Union County created a committee of fifteen men to draft a resolution objecting to the bill. It passed in Union Township 154 to 12 in 1840. Countywide the vote was 1,620 to 267.

As soon as Samuel was old enough—eight or so—he most likely worked for his father on the family's subsistence farm. When he was thirteen in 1834, a "black" frost hit the Buffalo Valley on May 31 and June 1. It was so cold that whole orchards of apples, pears, and cherries were killed. Bears looking for food came down from the mountains to feed on green corn and scores were killed by farmers. Birds survived and thrived, as caterpillars were prodigious.

Samuel went out on his own when he married Mary Ann Swartz, who had been born in nearby Juniata County in 1821. Juniata County was formed on March 2, 1831, from parts of Mifflin County. Nothing is known about Mary Ann's mother. All that is known about her family is that her father, John Swartz, was a native Pennsylvanian, born about 1794, and that she had a brother, John.

Samuel and Mary Ann were married somewhere between 1840 and 1843, when both were in their early twenties. They may have been married at the Lutheran and Reformed Church that was dedicated in Buffalo Township in 1839. We can deduce when they married because, in the 1840 census, Samuel was living with his mother and Mary Ann was living with her father in Union Township, Union County. Then in 1850, they were counted together in the census in Union County with three children; the oldest, John, was six. They had six more children: Emma, Jonathan, Matthew, Matilda, and twins Jane and Mary Louisa, who were born in 1858.

There were 242 families in Union Township in 1850 and a total population of 1,436. Nearly every family had its own home. There were 235 dwellings in the township. There was one merchant and two clerks at the township's only mercantile. There was one inn and one physician. Three men were employed as limeburners. There were a smattering of blacksmiths and wheelwrights, but eighty-five percent of the men worked as farmers or laborers, Samuel among them. In the mid-nineteenth century, there was plenty of labor to be done in Central Pennsylvania. Forested land had to be cleared for the building of settlements, roads, rail beds, gristmills, dams, and canals. Much of the money for such projects came from lotteries. The Union Canal lottery was conducted in 1826. Sometime in the 1850s Samuel and Mary Ann moved east to Mifflin Township in Dauphin County, where Peters was a common surname. Peters Mountain runs for thirty miles in central Dauphin County.

Dauphin was further east and closer to the roads and rail lines to Philadelphia, York, and Harrisburg than Union. Dauphin had been settled earlier and was more progressive, more populated, more developed and richer than Union. For example, Dauphin had a good school system, with nine one-room schoolhouses, as early as 1830. It is likely Samuel and Mary moved for better work opportunities for Samuel, but the existence of good schools may also have been a lure. Perhaps Mary, who could not read and write, wanted better for her children. It is known that Jonathan and Tillie, at least, went to school in Dauphin.

In 1860, Samuel was still working as a laborer at a time when there was even more work available. The anthracite coal industry was heating up in Dauphin County. Though it is believed Samuel never worked directly for a coal company, the industry created peripheral work. Better road and railroads were needed for the industry. Homes, churches, and schools were needed in the boroughs for the immigrant mineworkers. Samuel could have worked as a laborer for farmers, road builders, carpenters, or stonemasons. The farmers also benefited from the better roads and railroads as they moved from subsistence farming to the commercial farming of food for cities. Philadelphia was having a growth spurt of its own, and could not feed itself. Dauphin County provided commercial quantities of wheat, corn, linseed oil, rye, and whiskey. The Civil War build-up—which began when Lincoln was reelected President in November—and the war itself also increased economic activity and work.

During the war, Samuel went to Perry County, a small county that bordered Dauphin at the Susquehanna north of Harrisburg in the Millersburg area. It's not known what Samuel was doing in Perry County. Had he gone there to work? Had he and Mary split? What is known is that he died there in about 1865 and that before he left Dauphin he and Mary had one last child, Mary Louisa. Perry wasn't far from Samuel's home in Dauphin by rail or from where he grew up in Union by ferry. He was only 44 and may have been in Perry working or he may have been ill and staying with relatives. He was buried in Perry County.

Mary Ann outlived Samuel by thirty-two years. After his death she moved to the Lykens area and worked as a housekeeper. In the 1880s she retired and moved in with her daughter, Jane, and her husband Alfred Row in Washington Township, Dauphin County. She was seventy-five when she died in 1897 of heart disease. She was buried in St. Johns Oakdale Cemetery, Loyalton. Samuel and May left a legacy—family. Their *caboose* Mary, one of the twins they had in their late thirties, turned out to be the direct line to the Thompson family.

DAVID M. WERT & CATHERINE SHOOP

David Wert was the son of parents who bucked the odds. His father, Jacob Wert, and mother, Sarah Faber, both native Pennsylvanians, were born in 1804 and 1807, respectively, when the average life expectancy was forty-five years. Sarah, the daughter of John Faber and Maria Rudy, lived to ninety-five. Jacob, the son of John Wirth and Anna Miller, lived to eighty-four. Because records were hand-written in the early eighteenth century, different spellings of last names were not unusual.

Though not as long-lived as his parents, David did live to seventy-one, a longer-than-average lifespan in the nineteenth century. During his life, David worked as a laborer, was married twice, and fathered fourteen children. But it was one of the ten children he had with his first wife, Catherine Shoop, who is of most interest here.

David was born in Powells Valley, Dauphin County, Pennsylvania, on April 1, 1829. David was the oldest of nine siblings, followed by Elizabeth, Catherine, Sarah, John, Adam, Peter, Matthew, and Martha. He died two years before his mother on December 9, 1900, in Dayton, Dauphin County, Pennsylvania, of lung congestion. He was buried from the Calvary United Methodist, or Union, Church in Wiconisco, Dauphin County. Wisconisco was laid out in 1848. The church was erected in 1854.

David married Catherine Shoop about 1849 in Dauphin County. He was twenty and she was nineteen. Catherine was the daughter of John Shoop and Sarah Wertz. Catherine was born on February 24, 1830, in Northumberland County, which borders Dauphin to the north. Catherine was baptized on March 6, 1830, in the Stone Valley Reformed Lutheran Church, also known as Zion Church, in Northumberland County. The church was established in the 1770s. She was the second oldest of four girls. Her older sister was Anna Shoop and her younger sisters were Anna Maria, Elizabeth, and Salome, or Sarah.

David and Catherine probably met at a church function or through relatives. In any case, they didn't live far apart. Catherine was counted in the census in 1830 and 1840 with her father in Lower Mahanoy, Northumberland County, which was about ten to fifteen miles from Halifax, Dauphin County, where David was counted in the census in 1830 and 1840 with his family.

After they married, David and Catherine moved to Upper Paxton, Dauphin County, which was right between their families' homes in Halifax and Lower Mahanoy. They most likely moved for work, though being equidistant from their families was a plus. Upper Paxton was bordered by Mahantango Mountain to the north, Berry Mountain to the south, and the Susquehanna River to the west. The nearest town, Millersburg, was an important ferry town on the river. The area was rich with timber, streams, and wildlife. As a laborer, David might have worked building roads, laying rail, and digging canals, though more likely as a farmer. They lived in Upper Paxton in the early 1850s, but in the late 1850s, they moved to her home area of Lower Mahanoy, Northumberland County. David was not drafted during the Civil War—though he was well within age, being thirty in 1860); he was married with four children under age six, and that may have been a factor.

Perhaps prompted by Catherine's father's death in 1859, David and Catherine moved again to the Lykens area of Washington Township in Dauphin County, where they were counted in the census of 1870. By then they had all of their ten children: Elizabeth, Anna, John Henry, Mary, Melinda, Martha, Catherine, Amelia, Daniel, and Isaac. David likely worked as a farm laborer for one of their neighbors. There was plenty of work—the area was booming economically with the growth of the anthracite coal industry. Immigrants were moving to the area to work the mines and they had to be fed, clothed, and housed. Also, commercial farming was growing as families moved into the cities following the Civil War, where they were more likely to buy food than to grow it. This was the beginning of a trend that would accelerate with the Industrial Revolution.

Recreation in the Dauphin area in the eighteenth century revolved round family, church, neighborhoods, organizations such as the Grange, and work. Families gathered at holidays, churches held socials, neighbors got together to build barns and Granges, and workplaces threw picnics with games for kids and adults.

Catherine died on June 8, 1872. She was buried from St. Peters Reformed Lutheran Church, also known as the Hoffman Church, in Loyalton, Dauphin County, near Lykens. After Catherine's death, David moved by himself to Union Township, Berks County, where he was counted in the 1880 census as a boarder of Winfred Allison, a widower with three young children.

Son John, then fifteen, went to live with Jacob and Elizabeth Seiler in Jackson

Township, Northumberland County. His sisters Martha and Catherine lived with families in the Lykens area as maids or servants. By 1900, David and second wife, Elizabeth Bellis, moved back to Washington Township, Dauphin County.

The many place names mentioned above might leave the impression that the families traveled widely in the eighteenth century, but they didn't. Powells Valley, Stone Valley, Upper Paxton, Lower Mahanoy, Lykens, Washington Township, Jackson Township, Wisconisco, Halifax, and the counties of Dauphin, Northumberland, and Union are all within five to twenty-five miles of each other and the larger Lykens Valley area.

The climate was moderate with plenty of rain. All the areas had similar landscapes of lush valleys and rolling mountains of hardwood trees—such as oak, chestnut, hickory, and beech—and softer woods like white pine. But these landscapes changed during David's lifetime. When Europeans first explored the area, trees covered more than 90 percent of Dauphin County's 400,000 acres. But steel plows and axles allowed European settlers to quickly clear large areas of forest for subsistence farming. There were probably one thousand subsistence farms in Dauphin County by 1860. In the later part of the century, clear-cutting to lay out towns and facilitate mining destroyed large swaths of forest. By the 1850s, Pennsylvania was the nation's largest supplier of lumber and other wood products such as wood alcohol and tannic acid from hemlock, used to process hides. By 1900, the year David died, Dauphin had lost more than 60 percent of its forests. Rain washed soil from the clear-cut areas into streams, and forest fires burned through the dead stumps, dry branches, scrub brush, and saplings, ruining fish and wildlife habitat.

The Europeans saw the forests as dollar signs and as an impediment to development. Little attention was paid to the negative effects of clear-cutting until the Pennsylvania Commission of Forestry was founded in 1901. After World War I, many rural Pennsylvanians moved into the cities and abandoned farms were reforested.

David Wert was not one of those who moved to a city, though by 1890s—when he moved to Lykens—it was a well-developed area due to the economic spillover of the anthracite industry. David was still working as a laborer right up until his death in 1900. It was David's son John Henry who was the direct ancestor of the Thompson line.

DANIEL ROW & SUSAN FRANTZ

Daniel Row was born on July 10, 1813, in Dauphin County, Pennsylvania. Though the War of 1812 was being fought at the time, it had no impact in Dauphin County. The only Pennsylvania Battle was on Lake Erie, where Captain Perry defeated the British two months after Daniel was born.

Daniel was the third child of Barbara Rudy and John William Rowe. His older siblings were Wendell and Jacob. His younger siblings were Susan, John, Elizabeth, Sarah, and Joseph. Daniel lived to age fifty-eight. He died on July 31, 1871, in Dauphin County. Though that was a fairly long life for the time, he was outlived by both his parents. His father, John, was born in June 1785 in Strasburg, Lancaster County, Pennsylvania, and lived to age ninety-two, dying in 1877 in Berrysburg, Dauphin County. Daniel's mother, Barbara, was born in April 1796 also in Strasburg. She died at age eighty-five on December 15, 1881, also in Berrysburg, Dauphin County.

Daniel's parents migrated to Dauphin from Strasburg soon after they married, probably around 1810. The Strasburg-Lancaster area was more developed than Dauphin County, which was an area of forests pockmarked by subsistence farms.2 It is likely Daniel and Susan moved for the adventure—a desire to strike out on their own and for land—perhaps urged on by relatives who were already in Dauphin. It wasn't an easy journey. Though only 75 miles, the journey likely took a week to ten days by Conestoga wagon, stagecoach, or on foot or horseback.3 They may have been in a caravan of settlers traveling on dirt roads that were little more than widened Indian trails passing through the Blue, Second, and Peters Mountains. In any case, when Daniel was born, they were in Dauphin in the Halifax area. John was working as a farm laborer.

Daniel married Susan Frantz, a native of Dauphin County, in the late 1830s when she was in her late teens and he was twenty-five. This is evident because both were living with their parents in 1830 and they were together in 1840. Susan Frantz was born March 23, 1819. She was named for her mother, Susan Giesemen, who was born in 1787 in Tulpehocken, Berks County. Her father, Adam Frantz, was born in 1780 in Lykens, Dauphin County. She was the third youngest of their eight children. Her older siblings were William, Jacob, Catherine, John, and Christina and her younger siblings were Sarah and Samuel.

Unlike her husband's parents, Susan's parents died young. Her father was in his forties when died between 1825 and 1830 in Dauphin County. Her mother was forty-nine when she died in 1826. It was a fate that would also befall Susan. She died in 1861 at age forty-two, with four young girls—Susan, Amelia, Leah, and Adeline—still living at home. The girls were four of the seven children of Daniel and Susan. Their older siblings were Sarah, Angeline, and Adam, the lone son.

After Susan's death, the family scattered. In 1870, Daniel—who would die within a year—was living with Jacob Zerber in Berrysburg and still working as a laborer. Daughter Susan was eighteen and working as a cook in a boarding home near Berrysburg. Amelia was living with David Matter, a successful farmer in Washington Township with a farm valued at $11,500—the equivalent of $500,000 today. Leah was living with John Lebo, a butcher in Lykens. Adeline was just three doors away living with her aunt Susan Ely and attending school.

Daniel never attended school and was illiterate, not an unusual circumstance for men of his generation who worked farms in rural Pennsylvania. But Daniel had a descendant who was different. Daniel's nephew, Jonas Row, was his brother Jacob's son. Jonas was one of the most interesting members of the extended family. Jonas was a farmer, yes, but he attended school. Over the years, he was active in politics and was a supervisor of roads, a tax collector, and a justice of the peace. He was also a butcher and a merchant. Somehow he found time to be a deacon, trustee, and Sunday-school superintendent and teacher in the Lutheran Church.

During the Civil War in 1863, Jonas enlisted in the Union Army at Harrisburg. Assigned to the One Hundred and Twenty-seventh Regiment, Pennsylvania volunteers, under Colonel Jennings and Captain Bell, he participated in the battle of Gettysburg and was wounded in the knee. He was discharged after only three months' service. Though the wound left him lame him for life, it didn't stop him from re-enlisting in the fall of 1863. With Company F, Sixteenth Pennsylvania, he was at Petersburg for five days, where bravery in action got him promoted to the rank of Orderly to General Gregg. Jonas was at the surrender of General Lee, and was mustered out of service in 1865.

After the war, he bought fifty-five acres and sunk $5,000 into developing a farm. He took a loss on that farm after using it as security for a loan for a friend. But again, he was not stopped from achieving his goals. He bought another eighty acres in Jefferson Township near Lykens and built a successful farm. Well-known and highly respected, he died in Schuylkill County at the age of eighty-two.

Daniel died in July 1871 of Bright's disease, a chronic inflammation of kidneys. For the first half of Daniel's life, the economy of the Lykens Valley area of Dauphin County was subsistence farming and the few peripheral businesses needed to support the farms, such as blacksmiths and limeburners, who burned limestone to create lime for fertilizer. There was very little commerce. Three things changed that in the second half of Daniel's life: the growth of the anthracite coal industry, the Civil War, and the emergence of the industrial revolution. Improved roads, the Pennsylvania canal system, and rail lines connected the area to the outside world. Timber, coal, and farm products became valuable commodities. Money replaced barter and banks were established in the towns such as Lykens, Berrysburg, and Elizabethville. Daniel was always counted as a nonspecific laborer in the census reports during his adult life. Though he wasn't a union miner or railroader, it's not hard to imagine him doing any or all of the necessary down-to-earth labor the modernization of Dauphin County required. There was plenty of work for a man with a strong back and a shovel.

Daniel was buried from the St. John's Lutheran Church in Berrysburg, Dauphin County, just as his wife, Susan, had been ten years earlier. Also known as the "Church of the Hill," it was the same church where Daniel was baptized in 1813. It was also the same church where generations of the extended family were baptized, married, and buried. The "Church of the Hill" had been built of stone on a hill overlooking the Lykens Valley in 1872, replacing a log church built in 1802. The parish roots dated back to 1773, when the Reverend J. Enderline, a pioneer missionary, came to Lykens Valley.

Daniel and Susan's youngest daughter, Adeline, was the direct line ancestor to the Thompson family.

WILLIAM GEHRHART HEINRICH DANKERT & MARIA CAROLINA HENRIETTE KELLING

William Gehrhart Heinrich Dankert, son of John Peter Dankert and Catharine Magdalena Westphals was born on December 13, 1797 in Gressow, Germany. He died about Abt. 1850 in Prussia. He married Maria Carolina Henriette Kelling, daughter of Nicholas Kelling and Anna Dorothy Koppelmann in 1817 in Germany.

Maria Carolina Henriette Kelling, daughter of Nicholas Kelling and Anna Dorothy Koppelmann was born on July 27, 1794 in Hohenkirchen, Mecklenburg-Schwerin, Germany. She died on January 31, 1865 in Hohenkirchen, Mecklenburg-Schwerin, Germany.

Maria Carolina Henriette Kelling and William Gehrhart Heinrich Dankert had the following children: Friedrich Heinrich Dankert, Margaretha Sophia Dorothea Dankert, Carl Johan Rudolph Dankert, Maria Sophia Dorothea Dankert, Sophia Dorothea Magdelena Dankert and John Frederick Dankert.

Little is known at this point about the Dankert family. The family lived in Prussia, now Germany, in the early 1800's. Typically this family would have farmed in a rural area. Their son John Frederick Dankert left his homeland alone about 1865, immigrated to America and settled in Sunbury, Pennsylvania. As an American, Frederick *became* a Duncan and was the direct ancestor of the Thompson line.

DAVID MCCLOUD & MARY ZERFASS

David McCloud was born around 1807 to John McCloud, probably in Northumberland County Pennsylvania, where he lived most of his life and married his wife Mary Zerfass. The couple married sometime around 1835. David was 28 and Mary was twenty years old.

The young couple married in Augusta, one of the seven original townships established in Northumberland. The seven townships created in 1772 were Augusta, Eagle, Buffalo, Penn's, Turbot, Wyoming, and Muncy. The townships were divided and subdivided, into new townships and counties, as the population of the area grew. Augusta was divided into Upper and Lower Augusta in 1846.

Augusta and Turbot are the only townships of the original seven that are still in Northumberland County. Sunbury remains the county seat. It is believed that David may have grown up in Augusta. One of the earlier censuses shows David living in Augusta with his parents, who were in their 70s or 80s. David was 23 at the time of this census.

Pennsylvanians of that time were extremely patriotic and had a well-organized militia and navy. They played a dominant role in the Revolutionary, 1812 and Civil wars. David was still young when the War of 1812 broke out, but as he grew up he surely heard stories of how Pennsylvanian General Jacob J. Brown successfully defended Sackets Bay from a British invasion in 1813; or how Oliver Hazard Perry won the Battle of Lake Erie with his fleet of ships built at Erie by native Pennsylvanian Daniel Dobbins.

Listening to these fire-ring stories from the older men may have inspired him to seek employment in the nautical industry as he grew up. During the early nineteenth century small steam boats and some sail boats were the main transportation for people and commodities such as coal from the Wyoming basin, located in northern Northumberland County, to other communities along the Susquehanna River. David may have worked on a boat or ferry in the county's extensive canal system at this time, or possibly as a laborer in one of the shipping yards along the Susquehanna River in Augusta.

The State of Pennsylvania spent a great deal of money constructing canal systems between Shamokin Dam, Sunbury, Northumberland, and adjacent points.

Similar facilities were provided on the West Branch, and also on the division between Northumberland and Harrisburg.

During the prosperous days of the canal, Northumberland was an important point on the water highway. Two packet boats, the George Denison and Gertrude, were launched in 1835 for the express purpose of transporting people between Northumberland and Wilkes-Barre. Although, hundreds of thousands of dollars were collected in annual tolls, the State Public Works never made their money back on the canal systems.

Shortly after the couple married, the railroads made the canal systems almost obsolete. To avoid further expenses with maintenance and repairs, the State sold the main line between Philadelphia and Pittsburg to the Pennsylvania Railroad Company, and the West Branch division was sold to the Philadelphia and Erie Railroad Company. The North Branch division was sold to the Pennsylvania Canal Company and was used mainly to transport coal until later in the century.

As jobs on the canals became scarce, David may have gone to work for one of the railroad companies, active in Northumberland County. Another thought is that David may have worked in the abundant coal fields of the area. The first coal was marketed from the Shamokin coal basin, just across the Shamokin Creek from Augusta, in 1814. From then on Pennsylvania, particularly Northumberland County became a major resource for coal in the nineteenth century.

By 1840, the couple had two children: Joseph, born in 1836, and Sarah, born in 1839. The couple went on to have seven more children: Mary Ann, born in 1844; Catherine, born in 1847, who became the Matriarch of the Thompson family; Daniel, born in 1849; Frederick, born in 1852; Jeremiah, born in 1853; Judith, born in 1855, and William, born in 1856. The couple moved around the area frequently, possibly following the opening of new coal mines or the extensions of the railroad. Hollowing Run and Sunbury were two of the towns the family lived in, although, they kept returning to Augusta.

They were counted as residents of Augusta in the 1830 and 1840 census and as residents of Lower Augusta in the census from 1850 through 1880. The latter of these census records show real estate owned by the couple valued at $100 in 1860 and $150 in 1870, so they must have owned a home there that kept bringing them back to Lower Augusta.

David passed away sometime before May 19, 1864. Mary was around 49 years old when David died. Their youngest children, Judith and William, were only around nine and eight. In the 1870 census, Jerry, Judith, and William were the only children still living with their mother. By this time, Catherine was already married and probably had all of her six children before her mother died, sometime between 1880 and 1890. David and Mary's fourth child, Catherine, was the direct ancestor of the Thompson line.

MICHAEL LAYMAN & ELMIRA ELIZABETH RAYMOND

Michael Layman was born in Marietta, Lancaster County, Pennsylvania, on October 10, 1818. He was the oldest of eight children born to Michael Layman and Sarah Klein. His father was born in Centre County, and his mother in Lancaster County. Michael, along with his brothers and sisters, Catherine, Christina, Elizabeth, George, Henry, Sophia, and David lived in Lancaster County for most of their lives.

Lancaster County was one of the seven original counties of Pennsylvania. Farming flourished in the rich carbonate soil with relatively little slope, moderate climate, and evenly distributed rainfall. Nearly two thirds of the county was farmland then and still is today.

Marietta began as a small Indian trading post in the early 1700s. By the 1820s Marietta experienced a cultural and economic boom. The construction of the Pennsylvania Canal at Marietta attracted entrepreneurs and made it easier for farmers to sell their crops for higher prices in cities like Philadelphia and Baltimore, and even downstream to New Orleans. The flatboat was popular with farmers of that time to transport their crops. The boats were only twelve to sixteen feet wide but could be as long as 100 feet. Steamboats and the railroads soon offered a quicker and less hazardous means of getting their crops to market.

As a child, Michael probably worked the family farm. He no doubt accompanied his father on one or more of the journeys transporting their crops to market. Corn, wheat, hay, tobacco, and vegetables were the main cash crop of the area. Michael and his father could load up to 1,500 pounds of crops on their flatboat, which could garn around $5,000 in the larger cities. That would be around $125,000 by today's standards, certainly a good payoff for the year's wages. As time went on, Michael became enchanted by a young woman in Elizabethtown, about nine miles from Marietta.

Elmira Raymond, daughter of John and Nancy Reiman, was born January 17, 1824, in Maytown, York County, Pennsylvania. John and Nancy probably changed the spelling of their last name to give their daughter an American spelling of the German name. At some point between Elmira's birth and when she met Michael, the family moved the six miles from Maytown to Elizabethtown. It's possible that John was also a farmer and bought a farm in the predominantly farming community of Elizabethtown.

John and the elder Michael may have been business acquaintances, partnering in the flatboat to take their crops to market. This could explain how the young couple met. With their families in the same business, Michael and Elmira may have had ample time to fall in love.

John and Nancy moved from Elizabethtown back to York County at some point, possibly to Lower Chanceford. Perhaps as John and Nancy saw the love kindling in their daughter, they wanted to avoid a marriage because of the different faiths of the families; Elmira's family was Lutheran and Michael's family was Methodist. Or maybe it was the age difference with Michael being six years older than Elmira that spurred the move. But true love cannot be kept apart.

Probably shortly after their move, John passed away in 1841 when Elmira was seventeen. Michael and Elmira surely kept in touch, writing love letters to each other. Michael was pledging his undying love and Elmira was torn between her love for Michael and not wanting to leave her mother alone.

As fate would have it, love always wins. The young couple was married on April 3, 1845, in Christ Lutheran Church in Elizabethtown with the approval of her mother. They most likely lived on the Layman family farm in Marietta after they wed. Elmira must have converted to the Methodist religion after her mother passed away—sometime after 1841—as she and Michael were both buried in the Bethel United Methodist Cemetery in Lower Chanceford.

Leaving her mother alone was undoubtedly a concern for Elmira. Two years after they married, Michael moved his young bride and their two children—Jacob, age one and Sarah, only a few months old—to Lower Chanceford so that Elmira could be closer to her mother. Michael and Elmira went on to have seven more children: Uriah, Mary, Elmira, Charles, Joseph (who is in the direct line of the Thompson family), Lillian, and Theodore.

An interesting point to note is that Charles married Margaret McKinley a cousin of William McKinley, the 25th President of the United States. McKinley served from March 4, 1897, until his assassination in September 1901, six months into his second term. He was the last veteran of the American Civil War to serve as president. McKinley was a national Republican leader; his signature issue was high tariffs on imports as a formula for prosperity, as typified by his McKinley Tariff of 1890. As the Republican candidate in the 1896 presidential election, he upheld the gold standard and promoted pluralism among ethnic groups. His campaign, designed by Mark Hanna, introduced new advertising-style campaign techniques that revolutionized campaign practices and beat back the crusading of his arch-rival, William Jennings Bryan. The 1896 election is often considered a realigning election that marked the beginning of the Progressive Era. Sadly, Sarah and Mary passed away while young, around 1950; possibly an accident took both young girls.

After moving to Lower Chanceford, Michael went to work for the Tide Water Canal Company, probably working the weigh lock on the canal. He worked there for three years and then began working as a boatman. There were many ferries in that area. With Michael's experience taking goods down and across the Susquehanna River, he had no problem finding a job. Since there were no bridges across the Susquehanna River at that time, ferries were the only transportation across the river.

Boatmen would load people, goods, and supplies onto the flat bottomed ferry on one side and use poles to maneuver the ferry to the other side, where everything would be taken off and a new load put on for the trip back across the river. Boatmen were well paid, usually receiving a portion of the toll paid to the ferry company. There were usually hotels, restaurants, and taverns on each side of the river to refresh the weary travelers.

In 1855, a bridge was built across the river by the York Bridge Company. This was a very exciting time for the people who lived in York Furnace and the surrounding area. The Lancaster Examiner of November 20, 1855, celebrated the opening of the bridge. The paper said that the York County people of Fawn, Lower Chanceford, and Peach Bottom would no longer be cut off from commerce in the winter, when the Susquehanna and Tidewater canal was closed and roads were bad to York. Now they could easily get to Lancaster to do their buying and selling.

However, the excitement was short-lived. The bridge was opened in October 1855, but on April 5, 1856, the strongest windstorm known up to that time blew down the four spans across the eastern channel. They were carried downriver, but the contractors retrieved the timbers and started rebuilding. It was completed—some say to the last few planks—when, in early February of 1857, a severe ice flood destroyed it and took it away. The bridge was not rebuilt after that.

Unrest was brewing throughout the state that abolished slavery in 1780. But it wasn't until 1850 that the last slave in Pennsylvania was freed. The workings of the Underground Railroad were becoming less secretive. Michael surely heard about the Christiana Riots—where freed black men dared to rise up against white slave owners looking for a runaway—in Lancaster County in letters from home and in the Lancaster Examiner.

There was more and more opposition to slavery among the white religious population. Now there was news of the Southern states wanting to break away from the North because of the outcry to end slavery. Michael was surely not surprised when Fort Sumter thundered the call to war in 1861.

Michael was probably one of the first to enlist in one of the five companies: Worth Infantry, York Rifles, Marion Rifles, Hanover Infantry, and the York Volunteers, organized in York County. He must have had reservations about heading off to war and leaving his children and pregnant wife. Their last child, Theodore, was not born until 1862, yet he knew he had to fight this war for his children's sake, and he left.

It must have been a frightening time for his children—hearing of the battles and watching the soldiers as they went marching by their home on the way to war—knowing that their father was out there somewhere. Jacob, just barely 15, was now the man of the house, and most likely went out to get a job and support the family. It was a terrifying time for the young family, but they all pulled together until their father and husband came home.

Michael went back to work as a boatman on the ferries when the war was over. However, he longed for the feel of dirt in his hands again. Before long, he was living in York Furnace on a piece of land in a large home and crops in the field. As the children started to go out on their own, Michael and Elmira began to take in boarders.

Michael and Elmira were getting older and perhaps thought to get out of the farming business. They moved to Shanks Ferry around 1880 and went into the hotel business. Life was good for them until their youngest son, Theodore, died at the age of 25. Elmira passed away the following year in 1888 and Michael joined her four years later. Michael and Elmira's seventh child, Joseph, was the direct ancestor of the Thompson line.

JACOB WARNER OBERLANDER
& SARAH ANN GIPE

Jacob Warner Oberlander was born to a German farming family in 1819, in Chanceford, York County, Pennsylvania. He was the sixth of twelve children born to Michael Baugher Oberlander and Maria Catherine Warner.

The Oberlander's farm was probably in the family for generations; possibly forged by Jacob's great-grandfather, Andrew Miller, from land given to him for his service in the Revolutionary War. He served in the York Pennsylvania Regiment.

The practice of awarding land as payment for military service had been a common practice in the North American British Empire. At the time of the Revolutionary War, Colonial governments—under the assumption that they would win—offered land to those who enlisted in the Colonial Army.

The farm was undoubtedly very large in order to provide for Jacob's eleven brothers and sisters: Catherine, Daniel, Peter, Samuel, Sarah, Elizabeth, Mary, Susan, William, Michael, and Christian. It is quite possible that Jacob's grandparents, Jacob Oberlander and Susan Baugher, also lived on the farm along with other members of the family, as was the German custom of the time.

Most of the farms of that time were 100-plus acres. Jacob's great-grandfather probably started the clearing-out process of the land that continued with his grandfather and father. Jacob himself surely cut down trees and pulled out stumps to prepare a new field. It wasn't until the 1850s that settlers in the southern counties of Pennsylvania had more than 50 percent of their property improved.

Agriculture was the main occupation of Chanceford residents during this time. Wheat, rye, corn, orchard fruits, and tobacco were big cash crops that were taken to markets as far away as Baltimore and Philadelphia, and on to the coast for export to European counties.

Few of the farmers in this time were fully self-sufficient. Garden crops and services were traded locally to sustain their existence in the area. Some of the farmers formed "farming districts" and would pool their produce and resources—such as wagons or boats—to make the most of their trips to the distant markets.

Agriculture passed through several phases before moving into the Industrial Age during the second half of the century. At first the land was cleared, then the fresh soil was planted and replanted until it would no longer produce. Then came the discovery that lime would replenish the soil.

The Oberlanders probably built a lime-kiln and hauled large limestone shipments from the river to their kiln, where they would burn it before plowing it into the fields. Soon they found that it was cheaper to buy the lime at the river already burnt and haul it back to their farm. Liming gave way to other fertilizers such as manure, guano, super-phosphate of lime, and other types of soil additives.

The Industrial Age brought railroads, mills, ironworks, and distilleries. This gave the farmers local access to machinery that helped them produce more with less effort. Distilleries turned corn and wheat into liquor, which brought a higher price than the raw product. Mills turned wheat and rye into flour for easier shipping. There were two flouring mills in Chanceford, belonging to Samuel Warner and A. S. Warner, possibly members of Jacob's mother's family.

In his early 20s Jacob married Catherine Margaret Gipe, daughter of John and Elizabeth Gipe. They had four children: John, Susan, Mary, and Elizabeth. Tragically, Catherine died shortly after Elizabeth's birth in 1854.

Shortly after her death, Jacob married Catherine's younger sister, Sarah Ann Gipe, on October 26, 1854. Sarah was around twenty years old when she married Jacob. The marriage was probably to provide care to Sarah's nephew and nieces, though possibly it was for love. Jacob and Sarah had their first child, Luther, in 1855 and they went on to have ten more children: Sarah, Edward, Adeline, Rebecca, Caroline, Samuel, Margaret, Emmaline, Barbara, and Jacob.

It's possible that Sarah's and Jacob's parents were friends. Keeping with the customs of his German ancestry he welcomed Sarah's mother into his home. Elizabeth is counted in the 1860 census along with Christian, Jacob's younger brother, as living with Jacob and Sarah. Elizabeth passed away in 1861.

Sarah must have been a strong woman—she cared for her mother up to the end. Undoubtedly, she helped teach the children the workings of the family farm. It was common for the children and women to help with the everyday chores of the farm. She comforted their fears while they listened to the cannon fire of nearby battles during the Civil War. Possibly she was a member of one of the women's anti-slavery coalitions prominent prior to the war.

She probably worked alongside her husband during harvest time. She helped him increase the family's personal property from $640 in 1860 to $1,500 in 1870. Still Sarah took the time to nurture her children. Rebecca and the other children admired Sarah for her strength and loved her for her compassion.

Working the farm and raising fifteen children took its toll on Sarah though. Sarah passed away just before Christmas, 1874. Jacob raised the children by himself. Rebecca was just sixteen and her youngest brother was nine. Jacob lived about 21 more years, probably working the family farm with the help of his older children. The farming industry was changing—machinery was in common use on most farms. This probably gave him more time to clear off additional land.

Jacob died just after Christmas, 1898. Jacob and Sarah's fifth child, Rebecca, was the direct ancestor of the Thompson line.

ELIJAH ANDERSON & CATHERINE BORDNER

Elijah Anderson and Catherine Bordner were lifelong residents of Snyder and Northumberland counties in Pennsylvania. Their lives spanned the greater part of the nineteenth century and, except for Elijah's service in the Civil War, they rarely if ever felt the need to travel far from home.

Elijah was the son of William Anderson and Catherine Arnold. William had been born in Lancaster County, and Catherine had been born elsewhere in Pennsylvania. Their son Elijah was born in Chapman, Union County—which later split into multiple counties, including Elijah's birthplace in what would become Snyder County. He was baptized at one month old at Botshafts Lutheran Church in Union County. Elijah's grandfather, William Anderson, was a Revolutionary War soldier—a private in Lancaster's 6th Regiment, 4th Company, 6th Class.

Elijah was William and Catherine's fourth child. His older brothers were George, John, and Peter. After Elijah in 1820 came yet another brother, Samuel—the fifth boy in a row. Finally, Catherine presented the family with two girls, Elizabeth and Mary.

Catherine's parents, John Bordner and Maria Emerich, had been born in Berks County, southeast of Harrisburg, but by the time of Catherine's birth and baptism, the family had relocated to Lower Mahanoy, a rural township in Northumberland County just across the Susquehanna River from Chapman. Catherine's grandfather, Jacob Phillip Bortner, was also a Revolutionary War soldier—a private in Northumberland's militia.

Catherine was one of thirteen children born to the Bordner family over a span of twenty-one years. Preceding Catherine were five brothers in a row—John, Jacob, Jonathan, Philip, and Peter—and two sisters, Mary and Elizabeth. After Catherine in 1817, came Annabelle, Joseph, Louisa, Isaac, and George.

Elijah and Catherine married in August 1843 in Lower Mahanoy. Elijah was twenty-three years old, and Catherine was twenty-six. Elijah and Catherine settled in Chapman, and keeping to the tradition of large families had nine children: Samuel, Mary, Susan, Sarah, Josephine, Emma, James, Evaline, and Catherine.

Eventually, Elijah and Catherine passed away only a little more than a year apart—Elijah on October 18, 1892, in Port Trevorton, and Catherine on December 13, 1893, in Chapman. They were buried together at St. Johns United Methodist Church in Port Trevorton.

While Catherine was more than busy enough bearing and raising their large family, Elijah made his living as a tailor. Throughout the 19th century, clothing manufacture underwent profound changes. In the early part of this period, most clothing—except finely and expensively tailored garments for the wealthy—was hand-stitched by women at home. The first American factory for ready-made clothing was established in New York City in 1831. The patenting of the first practical sewing machine, in 1846, led to the establishment of a large-scale industry in ready-made clothing, depending for the most part on poorly paid women working in sweat-shop conditions.30

It is unlikely that Elijah could have made a decent living by producing the sort of clothing that common people wore. He probably learned to custom-measure and hand-stitch expensive clothing for the more well-to-do citizens—both men and women—of his community. During one census, he is listed as a "retail merchant." This probably refers to some sort of shop in which Elijah tailored and sold the type of outer garments that most of his fellow Pennsylvanians could not afford.

Like so many men, the Civil War interrupted Elijah's life and career. In America's later wars, Elijah—at over 40 years of age and with nine children—would have been considered ineligible for service. In the Civil War, however, thousands of forty-year-old fathers found themselves in uniform.

The citizens of Pennsylvania played a huge role in the Civil War. More than 360,000 Pennsylvania men—more than from any other state except New York—served in the Union Army. Pennsylvania mustered 215 infantry regiments.31

In October 1862, Elijah became a private in the 172nd Regiment of the Pennsylvania Infantry, Company A, serving under Captain Mish T. Heinzelman. The 172nd Pennsylvania was a "draft militia," a result of the Federal Militia Act of 1862 that was signed by President Lincoln in July 1862. The Union Army had previously been made up entirely of three-year volunteers, who were paid fairly substantial cash bounties upon enlisting. The Act of 1862 ordered the states to institute a draft of able-bodied men ages 18–45 to serve in draft militias for nine months.

"State line" sentiment was common in Pennsylvania. That is, Pennsylvanians were far more loyal to their state than they were to the United States. They eagerly joined emergency militias to defend Pennsylvania, but they often refused orders to cross the border, and they certainly were uninterested in following Federal orders to invade the South.

In mid-October, Pennsylvania began to draft men into draft militias. The imminent threat of being drafted—and therefore not receiving the cash bounties of volunteers—encouraged more than 200,000 men to volunteer for regular regiments. Another 80,000—including Elijah Anderson—were drafted into draft militia regiments. Most drafted regiments were sent on garrison duty far from action, but they freed up volunteer regiments for battle.

Elijah—like nearly all of his fellow draftees—was an inexperienced, barely trained soldier. The men of the 172nd received their brief training at Camp Curtin near Harrisburg. During the war, more than 300,000 soldiers moved through Camp Curtin, making it the largest army fort in either the Union or Confederate sides.

For most of its nine months of active service, the 172nd was assigned to garrison duty at Yorktown, Virginia. Toward the end of Elijah's nine-month tour of duty, however, he found himself on the move, on foot and by railroad. Elijah and the 172nd took part in the later stages of the Peninsula Campaign in Virginia, the first large-scale Union offensive in the eastern theater of war. Then, joining the Army of the Potomac, the regiment took part in the pursuit of General Lee to Warrenton Junction, Virginia, from July 19th to 25th.

Fortunately, the 172nd was never in hot combat—the regiment lost thirteen men to disease, but none in battle. The regiment returned to Harrisburg and disbanded on August 1, 1863, one month after the Battle of Gettysburg, which had taken place just 80 miles south of the Anderson's home.

It was no doubt with great relief that Catherine welcomed home her forty-three-year-old husband. Elijah was surely pleased to resume his work as a tailor in place of his not-so-willing adventure as a soldier. He had seen more of the world than he had ever expected to and there is no evidence in the record that he ever again traveled beyond a circle bounded by Chapman, Port Trevorton, and Lower Mahanoy. Elijah and Catherine's seventh child, James, was the direct ancestor of the Thompson line.

ABRAHAM GAUGLER & KESIAH KELLY

Abraham Gaugler and Kesiah Kelly—his wife of 46 years—lived their entire lives in rural Snyder County, Pennsylvania. Census data through those years indicate residences in Chapman and Union townships and in unincorporated Port Trevorton, all adjacent to one another on the west bank of the Susquehanna River.

Abraham was the sixth child of George Gaugler, born in Montgomery County, and Maria Magdalena who had been born in Northumberland County and whose maiden is unknown. Abraham's older siblings were Maria, Sarah, Elizabeth, Christina, and John, and he was followed by George.

Kesiah's parents were William Kelly, born in York County, and Elizabeth Shaffer of Northumberland County. Kesiah was the oldest of ten, followed in order by Sophia, Mary, Uriah, Elizabeth, John James, John J., Caroline, Lucetta, and Hiram. Kesiah's grandfather, John Peter Shaffer, was a Revolutionary War soldier—a private in Berks County 6th Regiment, 5th Company.

Abraham was christened at the Botshaft's Lutheran Church in Chapman. In such a sparsely populated area, Abraham and Kesiah had likely known each other from early childhood. We can imagine them attending the same one-room schoolhouse to get the little bit of education they received—reading, writing, very basic arithmetic—and whispering to each other during services at the local Lutheran Church.

Port Trevorton, around which the lives of Abraham and Kesiah revolved, was a tiny farming hub when they were children. Later, as coal mines were developed in the Zerbe Valley, the Trevorton and Susquehanna Railroad was built to bring coal to the town. It crossed the Susquehanna River on a long bridge from Herndon to Port Trevorton, and the canal basin that was built for off-loading the railcars gave the newly prospering town its appellation of "port." However, the railroad route from the mines to Port Trevorton was only in use for fifteen years, and when the bridge was removed in 1870 Port Trevorton rapidly slid back into its sleepy ways.

Abraham made his living not on the railroad or at the port, but as a farmer. Agriculture in the 19th century was a tedious backbreaking occupation. Horse-drawn plows were used to break the soil and horse-drawn wagons brought produce to market.

In these years, Snyder County became more effectively connected to distant markets by Pennsylvania's growing canal and rail system. As a result, instead of subsistence farming, farmers were able to grow cash crops for markets throughout the nation and even in Europe.

The temperance movement had a substantial impact on Snyder County farmers. Growing rye for distilling into whiskey had been a profitable enterprise, especially after improved transportation facilitated getting whiskey to market. However, as the temperance movement decreased the demand for distilled products, farmers in Snyder County shifted production away from rye grains and emphasized production of corn, wheat, pork, poultry, potatoes, and butter.

Even in a rural community such Snyder County the national nightmare of the Civil War had a profound effect. Thousands of young Pennsylvanians—lured by patriotism and by cash bounties—had volunteered for the Union Army. Eighty-thousand more—including men up to the age of forty-five—found themselves drafted by lottery into draft militias to serve for nine-month terms. In October 1862— the month of the draft lottery—Abraham was a forty-two-year-old father of eleven living children. No matter how patriotic Abraham's sentiments may have been, it was probably with a great sigh of relief that he attended the public lottery and did not hear his name called. Instead, he remained at home on the farm growing foodstuffs to help feed the army and perhaps shifting some of his production into sheep, which were desperately needed to provide wool for uniforms.

Families in rural America in the 19th century were much larger than today's families, typically ranging from seven to twelve. The lack of reliable birth control methods played a role, but much of the trend toward large families was also intentional. In that time of rudimentary medical care and poorer nutrition and sanitation, parents expected that not all their children would live to adulthood. In rural areas in particular it was expected that surviving children would achieve their highest educational attainment at an early age and then go to work helping to support their families. As a result, families tended to have many children.

However, even in those times the family of Abraham Gaugler and Kesiah Kelly was exceptional. They had fifteen children, born over a span of twenty-two years. Kesiah's last child, Ella, was born when Kesiah was forty-seven years old.

Abraham and Kesiah's children were John, Adeline, George, Emaline, James,

Elizabeth, Lucetta, Isabelle, a daughter K. J., Sarah, Minerva, Alice, Anna, Caroline, and Ella.

The Gauglers' fourth child, Emaline, was known as Ella. Born in 1848, she was married in her mid-teens and died at just sixteen years of age. Twenty-three years later, the Gauglers' named their fifteenth child Ella. We can wonder whether they looked back with sadness at Emaline who died so young and decided to name their latest—and last—child in memory of her long-deceased older sister.

Another interesting thing to note about the Gauglers' children is the fact that three of their first five children were boys, but after that Kesiah gave birth to ten girls in a row. When Abraham passed away at the age of eighty, as a result of apoplexy—paralysis due to stroke— and he had been a widower for fourteen years. Kesiah was buried at St. Johns United Methodist in Port Trevorton and in 1900 Abraham joined her. Abraham and Kesiah's seventh child, Lucetta, was the direct ancestor of the Thompson line.

MICHAEL A. KEEFER
& MARGARET MATILDA BUCHER

Michael A. Keefer and Margaret Matilda Bucher were born, married, raised their family, and passed away all within the radius of a very few miles. The town of Sunbury, in Northumberland County, Pennsylvania, was the focus for all the events of their lives. The farthest they seemed to have roamed was to Upper Augusta, the rural township adjacent to Sunbury.

Michael was born in 1815, the son of Daniel Keefer and Evaline "Eva" Arnold. Both of Michael's parents were born in Berks County—70 miles as the crow flies southeast of Sunbury—but they were married in Northumberland County and made their lifelong home there.

Michael was the fifth child of eleven. First came Michael's three older sisters, Mary, Catherine, and Elizabeth. Michael and his twin brother, Samuel—the only boys in their entire family—were born next, to be followed by Anna, Juliana, Margaret, Matilda, Amelia, and Rosanna.

Margaret Matilda Bucher was born in 1827, when her husband-to-be, Michael Keefer, was just short of thirteen years old. For the first three decades of her life, she was commonly known as Matilda. During the nineteenth century, it was customary for the children of immigrant families from non-English-speaking parts of Europe to be called by their middle names. As the daughter of parents who were both of German extraction—with the surnames Bucher and Mantz—this custom would have applied to Matilda. Later, however, these people began to adopt the usage of immigrants from English-speaking nations and employ first names for everyday use. At this time, in around 1860, Matilda became more commonly Margaret.

Margaret's parents, John Bucher and Elizabeth Mantz, were both native Pennsylvanians. Six siblings preceded Margaret: George, Harriet, Martin, Charles, Henry, and William. Two more, Mary and John, followed her.

Michael and Margaret lived a relatively commonplace life, rarely, if ever, venturing far from home. At forty-seven years old, Michael was too old—by two years—to be required to take part in the Civil War draft lottery of 1862. However, participating in the grand events of history was part of both their families' heritages. Two of Margaret's grandfathers had served in the Revolutionary

War—Henry Bucher had been a captain; and Nicholas Mantz, a private, was listed as having been a prisoner of war. On Michael's side, his grandfather Peter Keefer had served in the 1st Pennsylvania Regiment.

Michael and Margaret were the parents of seven children. Their first, Margaret, was born in 1845. She was followed by Mary, Anna, Alice, Charles, James (the Thompson direct ancestor), and, in 1860, Emma.

The first settlement at the site of Michael and Margaret's hometown, Sunbury, had been a multi-ethnic Native American village called Shamokin.2 Early in the 18th century, Shamokin residents included Iroquois migrants from the north, Shawnee and Lenape retreating from the expanding white settlement of eastern Pennsylvania, and Native Americans from Virginia. In 1756, the British built Fort Augusta to provide protection for early British settlers in the Susquehanna Valley. The town of Sunbury was founded at the site in 1772, and it was in Sunbury that Michael and Margaret were born and lived their lives.

The censuses list Michael's occupation as "laborer," "farmer," and, in 1870, as "RR conductor." The primary industries of Northumberland County during Michael's lifetime were agriculture, timber, and coal mining. Timbering and coal mining required a steady supply of laborers so Michael may very well have spent some of his working life in those industries.

Farming had originally been a largely subsistence enterprise, but Pennsylvania's growing canal and rail systems had connected rural communities like Northumberland County to distant markets. During Michael's lifetime, cash crops included wheat, potatoes, corn, pork, and poultry. He listed "farmer" as his occupation in 1860.

The Pennsylvania Canal—the generic term for Pennsylvania's broad network of freight- and passenger-carrying rivers and canals—was under construction and use throughout the early part of the nineteenth century. A strong young man could easily have found work as a laborer in digging the canals, building locks, or working at docks where barges loaded cargoes of coal, fresh-cut timber, and agricultural products.

The Pennsylvania Railroad was founded in 1846 with main lines and spurs running between major cities, reaching into coal- and timber-producing regions, and eventually connecting with railroads and barge lines into other states.

The new railroads opened up vast parts of Pennsylvania for the first time. As the Pittsburgh Daily Morning Post wrote in 1854, "There are people now living in Pittsburgh who have traveled diligently for a whole week to reach Philadelphia. The same persons can now go from our city to the eastern metropolis between sunrise and sunset of a summer's day, without fatigue, and without occasion for stopping to eat more than one meal."

Michael could have found heavy manual labor in the construction of rail lines, though when he was in his mid-fifties—no doubt exhausted by years of labor—he found less backbreaking work as a railroad conductor. This job would likely have taken him from one end of the state to the other.

One of the great events of the Keefers' lifetime—whether they knew it or not—occurred in 1883 at the Sunbury City Hotel when the inventor Thomas Alva Edison installed the very first three-wire electric lighting system.

Margaret died at the age of seventy-two in 1899, and Michael followed her five years later at the age of eighty-nine. They were buried side by side in the Penn's Sunbury Cemetery. Michael's marker reads "Our Father. M. A. Keefer. Died Feb. 25, 1904. Aged 79 Y. I. M. & 8 D." Michael and Margaret's sixth child, James, was the direct ancestor of the Thompson line.

GEORGE CULIN LIVEZLY & ANNA MARIA KENT

George Livezly left his influential Philadelphia family, changed the spelling of his surname, and settled in rural Schuylkill County, Pennsylvania. His wife, Anna Kent, traveled even farther—and in an even more adventurous manner—to reach her husband-to-be.

George was the seventh child of Jacob Livezey and Eleanor Culin. George's elder siblings were Charles, John (who died very shortly after birth), John Culin (born the next year and named after his deceased brother), Sarah, James, and Mary. George was followed by Jacob. George's father was the son of yet another Jacob, a veteran of the Revolutionary War.

Sometime in the 1850s, when George was in his late 20s or early 30s, he decided to leave his family's home in Philadelphia—where they were prosperous and well regarded—and strike out for the hinterlands. The spelling of his name changed from "Livezey" to "Livezly." Although many surname variants were accidental or strictly due to clerk's individual spellings, this name change seems conscious and the 'l' is nearly in every spelling. Interestingly, however, it's only George Sr.'s family, not the case with any of his siblings, nephews or nieces, all who used Livezey or Livesay variants.

George made his way in the hatter's trade as he is listed in the censuses variously as a hatter, a hat dealer, and owner of a hat store. This would have been a thriving occupation as hats—from working men's caps to wealthy men's derbies and top hats—were an essential part of the male wardrobe in the middle of the 19th century.

As a dealer in hats—rather than as a craftsman who made them—George would have escaped the hatter's occupational hazard of mercury exposure. Hatters in Europe and America used mercuric nitrate to treat the fur of small animals for the manufacture of felt hats, which resulted in a chronic condition known as "hatters' shakes—leading to the popular expression "mad as a hatter". Though England banned the use of mercuric nitrate by 1900, American hatmakers continued to use it until at least 1941.

Anna Maria Kent was born in New Orleans, Louisiana, in 1834. Her father was John Kent, who was born in England. Anna's mother's name is unknown, nor is it known whether Anna had brothers and sisters. What is known is that Anna—while still a teenager—had become a Roman Catholic nun. This was often the destination for young girls whose mothers had died or whose parents were otherwise unable to care for them, and so this may have been young Anna's situation.

Anna was likely an Ursuline. The Ursuline Order had been established in New Orleans in 1727, caring for the sick and trying to convert the Native American inhabitants. The city was growing and the Ursulines were well established by 1850, when the census of that year listed sixteen-year-old Anna as a nun.

The sisterhood apparently did not appeal to Anna, as she is soon listed as a "runaway nun." Somehow she made her way to Ashland, Pennsylvania, where she met George Livezly. Southern Pennsylvania had long been industrialized, but the area around Ashland remained mostly wilderness, broken only by a hotel that had been built on the main wagon road through the area.

However, Ashland lies in the anthracite coal region, and by 1846 miners were developing coal seams in the area. More people, including George and Anna, were attracted by the commercial activity, and by the mid-1850s, with 3,500 citizens, Ashland had a post office and a church. As a hat dealer, George would build his business and eventually open a store. Sometime around 1852, George and Anna married. Though they would move to New Jersey in later years, they remained in Ashland for four decades, raising their children there.

Their first child was a son, John. Next came George Jr., who lived only a year or so. After came three daughters: Georgeann, Eleanor, and Emma Louisa, followed by a second George Jr., James, and Anna.

In the nineteenth century, it was extremely common to name a child after his grandfather. It was common for fathers to name their children—both boys and girls—after themselves. George Livezly named their second child George Culin, after himself. When baby George died—as many babies did in those days—George named the next child, a girl, Georgeann, a combination of "George" and "Anna." But George apparently still wanted a son named after himself; and when—after two more daughters—Anna gave birth to a boy, George proudly named the boy "George Culin Livezly."

In 1880, George and Anna still lived in Ashland, but by 1890 they had moved to Cumberland County in far southern New Jersey, where they spent the about ten years living with their son George Jr. George passed away sometime between 1900 and 1910, presumably in New Jersey. Anna relocated to Warren, Massachusetts with son George Jr. and died August of 1910, being buried in Brattleboro, Connecticut, just across the border. George and Anna's fifth child, Emma, was the direct ancestor of the Thompson line.

CHAPTER 7

❋

Generation Seven

Family, like branches in a tree, we all grow in different directions,
yet our roots remain as one.
—UNKNOWN

Our Seventh Generation includes Robert & Janet Thompson, David & Elizabeth Penman, George & Susan Gutman, Peter & Maria Brown, Andrew & Mary Hensel, Joseph & Susan Romberger, John & Elizabeth Updegrove, Jacob & Elizabeth Culp, Peter & Catherine Batdorf, John & Elizabeth Welker, John & Maria Peters, John & Anna Swartz, Jacob & Elizabeth Wert, John & Sarah Shoop, William & Barbara Row, Adam & Susan Frantz, George & Magdalena Dankert, Nicholas & Dorothy Kelling, David & wife McCloud, John & wife Searfoss, Michael & Sarah Leyman, John & Elizabeth Raymond, Michael & Catherine Baugher, John & Elizabeth Gipe, William & Catherine Anderson, Balthaser & Magdalena Bordner, George & Magdalena Gaugler, William & Elizabeth Kelly, Daniel & Evaline Keefer, Henry & Betsy Bucher, Jacob & Eleanor Livezey and George & Mary Kent, of the late 1700's in Pennsylvania, Louisiana, England, Scotland and Germany.

These 32 couples represent the seventh generation and will be honored in the upcoming Family History volume.

James Anderson

Lucetta Gaugler

Robert Thompson &
Lydia Goodman

Howard Hensel &
Clara Updegrove

James Keefer

Emma Livezly

Thomas Batdorf &
Mary Peters

John Wert
& Adeline Row

Citations

Gerald G Thompson, Middletown, PA, June, 2010.1 Shirley Mary Duncan, #1487170-1935, 11-29-1935, Snyder Co, PA, Department of Vital Records, New Castle, PA.

Gerald Gilbert Thompson birth record, #1170270-1935, 09-23-1935, Dauphin Co, PA, Department of Vital Records, New Castle, PA.

Harper Bruce Thompson birth record, #344701, #122649-07, September 1907, Schuylkill Co, PA, Department of Vital Records, New Castle, PA.

Harper B Thompson death certificate, #2501265, Department of Vital Records, New Castle, PA.

Harper B Thompson, Obituary, Harrisburg Patriot Newspaper, July 1981.

Thompson-Batdorf marriage record, Register of Wills, Clerk of Orphans Court, Dauphin Co, PA, 1935.

Samuel Peters, Descendants of John Peters, Evelyn S. Hartman.

Myrtle A. Batdorf birth certificate, January 1918, Department of Vital records, New Castle, PA.

Myrtle Thompson, Obituary, Harrisburg Patriot newspaper, 1983.

Myrtle A Thompson death certificate, #3455802, Department of Vital records, New Castle, PA.

Duncan family information, Jack Lehman, North Charleston, SC.

William Duncan, April 1978, PA, Social Security Death Index, www.familysearch.org.

Irvin Francis Duncan, Birth record, Northumberland Co County Courthouse, Register of Wills, Sunbury, PA.

Irvin Duncan, April 1978, PA, Social Security Death Index, www.familysearch .org.

Irvin Francis Duncan death certificate, #0030831, Northumberland Co, PA, Department of Vital Records, New Castle, PA.

Mary Lucetta Anderson, Memoranda, Bob Anderson, PA, rmorris@ptd.net.

Mamie Duncan, April 1989, PA, Social Security Death Index, www.familysearch.org.

Mamie Lucetta Duncan death certificate, #0078833, #069201, April 1989, Department of Vital Record, New Castle, PA.

Mamie Luzetta Anderson, #061660-1908, 04-13-1908, Northumberland Co, PA, Department of Vital Records, New Castle, PA.

Mamie L Duncan, Probate file, 47-89-85, microfiche, Montour County Courthouse, Office of the Reg and Recorder, Danville, PA, Norman Nicol, ndnicol@epix.net, Mar 2008.

Abel Thompson death certificate, #0506211, #133775-93, January 1918, Department of Vital Records, New castle, PC.

Thompson-Hensel Marriage, Office of the Register of Wills, Schuylkill County, PA, June 1904.

Abel Robert Thompson, WW I Draft Reg Cards, 1917–1918 Record, www.ancestry.com.

Abel R Thompson, Probate file, 1918, unnumbered original papers, 34pp, Schuylkill Co Courthouse, Schuylkill, PA, Norman Nicol, Apr 2008.

Gussie May Thompson death certificate, #0506187, #31982, March 1973, Department of Vital Records, New Castle, PA.

Gussie May Hensel, Funeral obituary, March 1973.

Gussie Mae Thompson, Obituary, Pottsville Repulbican, Pottsville, PA, March 28, 1973.

Gussie M. Thompson, Greenwood Cemetery, Tower City, Schuylkill Co, PA, John Barket, Tower City, PA, B-3-1.

Gussie M. Thompson, Reg of Will book, Book 145, pp578–82, May 27, 1950, probated Sept 11, 1973, Schuylkill Co Courthouse, Schuylkill, PA, Norman Nicol, Apr 2008.

Michael Goodman, Descendants of Michael Goodman, Evelyn S Hartman, deanh@voicenet.com.

Abel F Thompson, Bob Averell Family Tree, Entries: 7956, Updated: 2004-08-01 00:29:03 UTC (Sun), Contact: Bob Averell.

Lydia Mae Thompson, Obituary, Pottsville Repulbican, Pottsville, PA, Jan 18, 1983.

James Edward Batdorf death certificate, #0506183, #66234-39, August 1954, Department of Vital Records, New Castle, PA.

James Edward Batdorf, Church record, Rev. O.S. Moyer, Angie Eddy, Maple Grove Cemetery, Eluzabethville, PA, p 29.

James Edward Batdorf, United States WW II Draft Reg. Cards, 1942 Record, 2243624, www.ancestry.com.

James Edward Batdorf, Social Security numident record, application for SS-5, SSA, Nov 2006, Baltimore, MD.

Batdorf-Wert marriage record, Church record, Rev. O.S. Moyer, Angie Eddy, Maple Grove Cemetery, Elizabethville, PA, p 16.

Beulah I Batdorf death certificate, #0506188, #057537, June 1983, Department of Vital records, New Castle, PA.

Beulah Batdorf, June 1983, PA, Social Security Death Index, www.familysearch.org.

Beulah I Batdorf, Obituary, Harrisburg Patriot News, 1983.

John Peters, Peters family information, Evelyn S Hartman, deanh@voicenet.com.

Peter Batdorf, Descendants of Peter Batdorf, Evelyn S Hartman, deanh@ voicenet.com.

Duncan-Layman mariage record, #8855, Northumberland Co, PA, 1899, Northumberland Co County Register of Wills.

Wm Duncan death certificate, #0030852, #90924, Northumberland Co, PA, Department of Vital records, New Castle, PA.

Duncan family information, Stephanie Gormley.

Duncan-Layman marriage record, April 20, 1899, Edward C. Eisley.

Duncan-Layman marriage record, #8855, Northumberland Co, PA, 1899, Northumberland Co County Register of Wills, Sunbury, PA.

Duncan-Layman marriage record, #8855, Northumberland Co, PA, 1899, Northumberland Co County Register of Wills.

Lottie V. Willard, death certificate, File #29987, Reg #19, #3505042, February 1936, Department of Vital Records, New Castle, PA.

William Duncan, Pomfret Manor Cemetery, Sunbury, Northumberland Co, PA, NCHS, The Hunter House, Sunbury, PA.

Duncan household, 1900 United States Census, microfilm image, PA State Library. Died Sunbury, PA, Duncan family information, Stephanie Gormley.

Charlotte Layman, Duncan family information, Stephanie Gormley.

Anderson-Keefer marriage record, Northumberland Co, PA, Northumberland Co Register of Wills, #11421.

William Anderson, May 1969, PA, Social Security Death Index, www.familysearch.org.

William Morris Anderson death certificate, #0740733, #050910-69, May 1969, Department of Vital Records, New Castle, PA.

William M. Anderson, Cemetery records, Orchard Hills Cemetery and Memorial Park, Shamokin Dam, PA, Janet, Section 3, Lot 188.

Anderson-Keefer marriage record, July 15, 1902, Northumberland Co, PA, Northumberland Co Register of Wills, #11421.

Bible p, Marriage records, source unknown.

Memoranda, Bob Anderson, PA, rmorris@ptd.net.

Emma L. Keefer, Bible p, Birth records, source unknown.

Emma Louisa Anderson death certificate, #0740677, #53801-503, April 1963, Department of Vital Records, New Castle, PA.

Emma Louisa Keefer, Northumberland Co, PA, 1861–92, Zion Evangelical Lutheran Church, search.ancesry.com.

Emma Louisa Anderson death certificate, #0740677, #53801-503, April 1963, Department of Vital Records, New Castle, PA.

Emma L. Anderson, Cemetery records, Orchard Hills Cemetery and Memorial Park, Shamokin Dam, PA, Janet, Section 3, Lot 188.

William Morris Anderson, #0740733, #050910-69, May 1969, Department of Vital Records, New Castle, PA.

William Maurice Anderson, U.S. World War 1 Draft Registration Cards, No 1674, 3-27-0, Snyder, PA, 1917, www.ancestry.com.

Emma L. Anderson, Emma Louise Anderson, obituary, Sunbury newspaper.

Robert B Thompson death certificate, #0042512, #102079, Reg # 102, October 1907, Department of Vital records, New Castle, PA.

Robert B Thompson, Greenwood Cemetery, Tower City, Schuylkill Co, PA, John Barket, Tower City, PA, B-1-1.

Thompson family information, John L linden, jllinden@comcast.net.

Alexander Thompson, Schuylkill County, PA, p 1054.

Lydia B. Thompson, Greenwood Cemetery, Tower City, Schuylkill Co, PA, John Barket, Tower City, PA, B-1-1.

Bob Averell Family Tree, Bob Averell, raverell@carolina.rr.com, awt.ancestry.com.

Howard A.C. Hensel, #0036895, #63360, Reg # 66, June 1927, Department of Vital records, New Castle, PA.

Hensel family information, Victor Hensel, NJ.

Howard Andrew Carson Hensel, Howard Andrew Carson Hensel probate file, 1927, unnumbered orginal papers, 21pp, probated June 29, 1927, Schuylkill Co Courthouse, Schuylkill, PA, Norman Nicol, Apr 2008.

Clara M Hensel death certificate, #0042528, #37124, Reg # 29, March 1926, Department of Vital records, New Castle, PA.

Casper Hansel, Descendants of Casper (LaHentzelle) Hensel, Evelyn S Hartman, deanh@voicenet.com.

Batdorf Family information, Virginia Faust.

Thomas Batdorf, #0102590, #81400-17, 1916, Department of Vital records, New Castle, PA.

Mary L Batdorf, #0042526, #7?-23, 1924, Department of Vital records, New Castle, PA.

John Wert, #0042527, #95868-1303, 1924, Department of Vital records, New Castle, PA.

Adeline Row, St. John Evangelical Lutheran Church, Berrysburg, PA, Sara S. Neagley, Elizabethville, PA. 84 Mrs. Adeline Wert death certificate, #26162, #3457526, March 1921, Department of Vital Records, New Castle, PA.

Descendants of Frederick Adam Faber, Evelyn S Hartman, deanh@voicenet.com.

Johann Heinrich Friedrich Dankert, Ancestry.com. Germany, Select Births and Baptisms, 1558–1898 [database on-line]. Deutschland, Geburten und Taufen 1558–1898 Germany, Select Births and Baptisms, 1558–1898, Provo, UT, USA: Ancestry.com Operations, Inc., 2014. Original data: Germany, Births and Baptisms, 1558–1898. Salt Lake City, Utah: FamilySearch, 2013.

Catherine Duncan, Death certificate, Northumberland Co County Register of Wills, Sunbury, PA.

Duncan family information, Stephanie Gormley, PA, 1989.

Melinda Duncan, Cemetery record, Apr 1933, A genealogists Guide to Burials in Northumberland Co, PA, Vol I, Meiser & Meiser, 1989.

Sallie Duncan, Cemetery record, Apr 1933, A genealogists Guide to Burials in Northumberland Co, PA, Vol I, Meiser & Meiser, 1989.

Sarah Duncan, Baptisms of Infants, Zion Evan Luth Register, 1851–1892, Sunbury, PA, p41.

Hannah Artilla Duncan, Baptisms of Infants, Zion Evan Luth Register, 1851–1892, Sunbury, PA, p94.

Charley Duncan, Baptisms of Infants, Zion Evan Luth Register, 1851–1892, Sunbury, PA, p101.

Layman/Lehman family information, Files, NCHS, The Hunter House, Sunbury, PA.

Joseph Pierce Layman, death record, Illinois Statewide Death Index, 1916–1950, www.cyberdriveillinois.com/GenealogyMWeb/ODPHdeathsearch.

Joseph Pierce Layman, State of IL, Dept of Public Health, DVS, Reg #4976, Primary Dt #3104, Cook, IL, Feb 1924.

Lehman-Oberlander marriage, source unknown.

Rebecca Lehman (Layman) death certificate, #105066, Reg # 456, #3457529, November 1921, Department of Vital Records, New Castle, PA.

99 Lucetta Anderson death certificate, #0740660, #117712-223, November 1916, Department of Vital records, New Castle, PA.

Anderson family information, Stephanie Gormley, PA.

Bible p, Birth records, source unknown.

James P Keefer death record abstract, August 4, 1892, Edward C. Eisley.

Thompson family information, Jim Thompson, jbthompson@compuserve.com, pp 4–11.

Thompson family information, Films from 1993, Jane L Fouraker, Lancaster Co, PA.

Thompson family information, Jim Thompson, jbthompson@compuserve.com, pp 4–11 & Thompson family information, Irene C. Stearns, DeKalb, IL.

Isabel Penman, Vital records Index, British Isles, Intellectual Reserve Inc, 8/5/2010.

Thompson family information, Irene C. Stearns, DeKalb, IL.

Alexander Thompson, Schuylkill County, PA, p 668–669.

Alexander Thompson, Miners Journal, December 5, 1873.

Mrs. Thompson, Burial record, Miners Journal deaths, 1851.

Michael Goodman, Tower City, Porter Centennial, 1868–1968, p 188.

Michael Goodman, Obituatary, FROM 'THE WEST SCHUYLKILL HERALD', 03 JANUARY 1901, Jeffrey A. Brown, ntrprz@dmv.com.

Michael Gurtmann, "Pennsylvania, Births and Christenings, 1709–1950," index, FamilySearch (https://familysearch.org/pal:/MM9.1.1/V2NX-KXS : accessed 19 Nov 2014), Michael Gutmann, 12 May 1811; Christening, citing SAINT JOHNS LUTHERAN CHURCH NEAR BERRYSBURG,MIFFLIN TWP, DAUPHIN,PENNSYLVANIA; FHL microfilm 845111.

Michael Goodman death certificate, #1252, May 1901, Dauphin County Register of Wills, Harrisburg, PA.

Hensel-Workman marriage record, 1853, Register of Wills, Dauphin Co, PA.

Hensel family information, Dauphin Co Marriages, 1852–1855, CAGS.

Hensel family information, History of Michael Hensel (Hentzel) Sr. & His Related Families, R. Longtin-Thompson.

Andrew Gise Hensel death certificate, #0036891, #115081, Reg # 84, December 1908, Department of Vital records, New Castle, PA.

Andrew Gise Hensel, #0036891, #115081, Reg # 84, December 1908, Department of Vital records, New Castle, PA.

Daniel Updegrove death certificate, #1071, March 1899, Dauphin County Register of Wills, Harrisburg, PA.

Updegrove Family information, Updegrove Genealogy, PA State library.

Daniel Updegrove, Vital records, Dauphin County, p 26.

Mrs. Sarah Updegrove death certificate, #0042525, #81494, File 42, Reg 2193, July 1923, Department of Vital Records, New Castle, PA.

Welkers in the USA & Nulls from PA, Greg Welker, gwelker@chesapeake.net, awt.ancestry.com.

Baddorf Family, Gratz History, p 193.

Peter Batdorf, St. Peters (Hoffmans) Union Church, Burials.

Peter Botdorf, St. Peter's (Hoffman's) Union Church, Lykens, Dauphin Co, PA, Gert Mysliwski, gert@foothill.net.

Peter Batdorf, Hoffmans Reformed Church, Lykens Valley, Dauphin Co, PA, Historical & Genealogical, pp 227–8.

Peter Batdorf, Probate files, 1881, Affidavit Rep #5, Dauphin County Courthouse, Reg of Wills, Deborah Hershey, Elizabethtown, PA, Mar 2008.

Elizabeth Batdorf, Hoffmans Reformed Church, Lykens Valley, Dauphin Co, PA, Historical & Genealogical, pp 227–8.

Mary Peters death certificate, bk C, #945, 1897, Dauphin County Register of Wills, Harrisburg, PA.

Mary Peters death certificate, Dauphin County Register of Wills, bk C, #945, 1897, Harrisburg, PA, 140, bk C, #945, 1897, Perry County Historians.

Mary Peters death certificate, Dauphin County Register of Wills, bk C, #945, 1897, Harrisburg, PA.

Wert Family, Jonathan Wert.

David Wert death certificate, Dauphin County Register of Wills, bk E, #852, December 20, 1900, , Harrisburg, PA.

Shoop family information, Are you my cousin, Howard Ward, haroldw1@ juno.com, awt.ancestry.com.

Monn & Related Families, Danni Monn Hopkins, clueless@clnk.com, awt.ancestry.com.

David Wert (West) death record, Extract from County Death records, 1893–1906.

Wert household, 1870 United States Census, Dauphin Co, PA, PA State library microfilm.

Wertz family information, Bob Messerschmidt, Laurel, MD, SusanM4383@ aol.com.

Wertz family information, Cindi Grimm, Grimm@ruralife.net.

Daniel Row, Baptismal record, St. John Evangelical Lutheran Church, Dauphin Co, PA, p 64.

Rowe family information, Howard E Row, Dover, DE.

Daniel Rowe, St. John Evangelical Lutheran Church, Berrysburg, PA, Sara S. Neagley, Elizabethville, PA, 424 6M 24D.

Susanna Rowe, St. John Evangelical Lutheran Church, Berrysburg, PA, Sara S. Neagley, Elizabethville, PA.

Joh Heinr Dankert, Mecklenburg-Schwerin Volkszählung, 1819 Mecklenburg-Schwerin, Germany, Ancestry.com. Mecklenburg-Schwerin, Germany, Census, 1819 [database on-line]. Provo, UT, USA: Ancestry.com Operations Inc, 2007. Original data: Mecklenburg-Schwerin (Großherzogtum), Volkszählungsamt. Volkszählung 1819. Landeshauptarchiv Schwerin. 2.21-4/4 Bevölkerungs-, Geburts-,Konfirmations-, Heirats- und Sterbelisten.

Gerhard Wilhelm Heinrich Dankert, Deutschland, Geburten und Taufen 1558–1898 Germany, Select Births and Baptisms, 1558–1898 Ancestry.com. Germany, Select Births and Baptisms, 1558–1898 [database on-line]. Provo, UT, USA: Ancestry.com Operations, Inc., 2014. Original data: Germany, Births and Baptisms, 1558–1898. Salt Lake City, Utah: FamilySearch, 2013.

Sophia Magaretha Qualmann, Mecklenburg-Schwerin Volkszählung, 1819 Mecklenburg-Schwerin, Germany, Census, 1819 Ancestry.com. Mecklenburg-Schwerin, Germany, Census, 1819 [database on-line]. Provo, UT, USA: Ancestry.com Operations Inc, 2007.

Carolina Maria Henriette Kelling, Deutschland, Geburten und Taufen 1558–1898 Germany, Select Births and Baptisms, 1558–1898, Ancestry.com. Germany, Select Births and Baptisms, 1558–1898 [database on-line]. Provo, UT, USA: Ancestry.com Operations, Inc., 2014. Original data: Germany, Births and Baptisms, 1558–1898. Salt Lake City, Utah: FamilySearch, 2013.

Caroline Maria Henriette Kelling, Deutschland, Tote und Beerdigungen 1582–1958 Germany, Select Deaths and Burials, 1582–1958 Ancestry.com. Germany, Select Deaths and Burials, 1582–1958 [database on-line]. Provo, UT, USA: Ancestry.com Operations, Inc., 2014. Original data: Germany, Deaths and Burials, 1582–1958. Salt Lake City, Utah: FamilySearch, 2013.

David McCord, Family tree. https://familysearch.org/tree/#view=tree&person=935Q-7XG&section=pedigree, familysearch.org.

David McCloud, Probate files, 1864, Northumberland County Courthouse, Reg of Wills, Sunbury, Bk 5, p261, PA, Robyn Jackson, genealogylover@msn.com, 2008.

Jeremiah McCloud, Pennsylvania, Death Certificates, 1906–1924 forJeremiah McCloud, ancestry.com.

McCloud-Frye, Marriage, Northumberland County, SS, #2856, Register & Recorder, Sunbury, PA, Oct 1890, Market St, Sunbury, PA.

Michael Layman, Bethel ME Cemetery, p 151, Jerome K. Hively, Brogue, PA.

Elmira Layman, Bethel ME Cemetery, p 151, Jerome K. Hively, Brogue, PA.

Duncan family information, 1870 United States Census, York Co, PA, Roll M593-1468, p 545, Image 700, ancestry.com & Microfilm, PA State Library, Hbg, PA.

Overlander-Kipe marriage record, #662-59, Calender of Vital Records of the Counties of York & Adams.

Sarah Oberlander, Probate files, 1874, Rep 42, York County Archives, York, PA, Deborah Hershey, Elizabethtown, PA, Dec 2008.

Casper Arnold, Crossley/Gunsallus/Kimmel Family, Worldconnect Project, worldconnect.rootsweb.com.

Anderson family information, Jim Anderson, Ontario, CAN.

Elijah Anderson, January 1820, Record of Grubb's (Botschaft) Lutheran Church, 1792–1875.

Elijah Anderson, Tombstone Incriptions of Snyder County, PA, M.B. Lontz, 1981.

Arnold family information, Snyder County pioneers, Snyder County.

Family Ties, Laurie Lendosky, llendosky@cyberia.com, awt.ancestry.com/cgi-bin/igm-cgi.

Cath. Anderson, 1893, Tombstone Inscriptions of Snyder County, PA, M.B. Lontz, 1981, Union County Historical Society.

Catherine Anderson, Letters of Adminstration, 1893, Snyder County Courthouse, Register of Wills.

Anderson family information, Stephanie Gormley, PA & Descendants of Philip Jacob Bordner, John Getz, jgetz@iu.net.

Croce/Walker Family Tree, Sue Walker, smawalker@comcast.net, awt.ancestry .com.

Abraham Gaugler death certificate, August 1900, Snyder County Register of Wills, Middleburg, PA.

Abraham Gaugler, Obituary, Middleburg Post, Thu Aug 30, 1900, c/o Pat Smith, pms9848@hot-mail.com.

Some of my ancestors, David A. Miller, david.miller@nwa.com, awt.ancestry .com.

Kelly family information, Sue Dufour, sdufour@skyenet.net.

Kesiah Gaugler, Mount Zion United Brethren Church Cemetery, Snyder Co, PA, Shaffer & Arnold, 1904, www.rootsweb.com.

Mrs Annie Duttry, Pennsylvania, Death Certificates, Ancestry.com. Pennsylvania, Death Certificates, 1906–1963 [database on-line]. Provo, UT, USA: Ancestry.com Operations, Inc., 2014.

Gougler/Thursby family information, Jean Doherty, jmd17601@yahoo.com.

Kieffer family information, www.geocities.com/jimmyk418/surname.htm.

Family of Eldon G. Keefer, Eldon G. Keefer, PeterKeefer@aol.com, awt.keefer.com.

Kieffer family information, Family Group record, Jere S. Keefer, Mercersburg, PA.

M.A. Keefer death certificate, February 1904, Northumberland Co County Register of Wills, Sunbury, PA.

Michael A. Keefer, Spruce St. Cemetery, Sunbury, Northumberland Co County Historical Society.

Keefer, Kiefer file, Northumberland Co County Historical Society, Sunbury, PA, Floyd, p 346.

Margaret M Keefer death certificate, April 1899, Northumberland Co County Register of Wills, Sunbury, PA.

Margaret M. Keefer, Spruce St. Cemetery, Sunbury, Northumberland Co County Historical Society.

Margaret M Keefer death record abstract, April 1899, Edward C. Eisley.

Margaret M Keefer death record, May 6, 1899, Northumberland Co County Register of Wills, PA, Sunbury, PA.

Margaret M Keefer, Obituary, Sunbury newspaper, Robert C. Eisley.

Michael A. Keefer, Spruce St. Cemetery, Sunbury, Northumberland Co County Historical Society.

Michael A. Keefer, Keefer, Kiefer files, Northumberland Co County Historical Society, Sunbury, PA.

Keefer family information, Family of Eldon G. Keefer, Eldon G. Keefer, PeterKeefer@aol.com, awt.keefer.com.

The Livezey Family, Sixth Generation, The Livezey Association, p 152.

Anna M Livezly, Death record, 388, Aug 1910, Warren, Massachusetts, Connie Taylor [connieataylor@icloud.com].

Livezty household, 1900 Census, "Livetzly" household, 1900 United States Federal Census, SD 6, ED 147, Sheet 12, Cumberland, NJ, www.ancestry.com & Microfilm, PA State Library, Hbg, PA.

Livezty household, 1900 United States Federal Census, SD 6, ED 147, Sheet 12, Cumberland, NJ, www.ancestry.com & Microfilm, PA State Library, Hbg, PA.

Robert Thompson, Ancestry Publci trees, O'Brien Family Tree, Owner: christine hillstead, ancestry.com.

Thompson family information, Jane Fouraker, mjfour@mindpsring.com.

Robert Thompson, Thompson History, Jim Thompson, jbthompson@compuserve.com, pp 4–11, Thompson family information, John B. Linden, Lynden@comcast.net.

Penman family information, Jim Thompson, jbthompson@compuserve.com.

David Penman, FHL, Pedigree chart, www.ancestry.com.

David Penman, Penman family information, John Penman, PenmanJC@ aol.com.

John Penman, Vital records Index, British Isles, Intellectual Reserve Inc, 8/5/2010.

Goodman family data, DESCENDANTS OF GEORGE GOODMAN OF BETHEL TOWNSHIP, BERKS CO, Lawrence Goodman, lawrenceeg@ comcast.net, http://www.goodmangenealogy.com/1104.htm.

Michael Gudman, Bethel. January 25, 1810. http://berks.pa-roots.com/.

Peter Brown, Tyson Family_2012-03-18, Owner: Gary Tyson, ancestry.com.

Brown family information, Peter Brown descedants, Deb Kandybowksi, debkandy@epix.net.

Andreas Hansel, Baptism, York Co, PA library, cards on file.

Andrew Hensel, Christ Church, Littlestown, PA, Adams Co County 18th records lookup, Virginia, vperry1@shawneelink.net.

Andrew Hensel, Death of an Old Soldier, Obituary, New Bloomfield newspaper, July 1875.

Andrew Hensel, Source 146, index card, Perry County Historians.

Mrs. Hensel, Source 140 & 146, index cards, Perry County Historians.

Mrs. Mary Hensel, New Bloomfield Times, January 20, 1877.

Mary Hensel, U.S., Find A Grave Index, 1600s, Ancestry.com. U.S., Find A Grave Index, 1600s–Current [database on-line]. Provo, UT, USA: Ancestry.com Operations, Inc., 2012. Original data: Find A Grave. Find A Grave. http://www.finda grave.com/cgi-bin/fg.cgi.

Workman family information, Evelyn Hartman, Evelyn S Hartman, deanh @voicenet.com.

Joseph Workman, Wiconisco Calvary Cemetery, Rhonda, yeahbaby@penn.com, Row 4.

Joseph Workman, U.S., Find A Grave Index, 1600s, Ancestry.com. U.S., Find A Grave Index, 1600s-

Current [database on-line]. Provo, UT, USA: Ancestry.com Operations, Inc., 2012. Original data: Find A Grave. Find A Grave. http://www.findagrave.com/cgi-bin/fg.cgi.

ibid.

The Romberger Line, Ancestors of Richard Alan Lebo.

Romberger Family, St. John's Lutheran Church, p 10, John Romberger.

Johann Uptegrav, 1805, Jacobs Church, Pine Grove, Swedberg, SCUR III, p 240.

Updegrove Family information, Rosie Byard, rbyard@bigfoot.com.

John Upderove, Smith Family Tree, Owner: hannibal8901, ancestry.com.

Rutzel Family Genealogy, David Rutzel, leztur@hotmail.com, awt.ancestry.com.

Elizabeth Reiss, Provizzi Family Tree, Owner: sprovizzi, ancestry.com.

Kulp family information, J. Wagner, Union County.

Mrs Elizabeth Kulp, Pennsylvania and New Jersey, Church and Town Records, 1708–1985 about Mrs Elizabeth Culp. Source Citation: Historical Society of Pennsylvania; Historic Pennsylvania Church and Town Records; Reel: 234.

Peter Batdorf, Descendants of Peter Batdorf, Evelyn S. Hartman.

Valentine Welker, Direct Descendants of Valentine (Welcher) Welker, Evelyn S. Hartman.

Dauphin County Names, Data p, Robert M Howard, www://genealogy.lv/ howard/.

Welker family information, Roger Cramer, rogercubs@aol.com.

John Welker, U.S., Find A Grave Index, 1600s-Current, Ancestry.com. U.S., Find A Grave Index, 1600s-Current [database on-line]. Provo, UT, USA: Ancestry.com Operations, Inc., 012. Original data: Find A Grave. Find A Grave. http://www.findagrave.com/cgi-bin/fg.cgi.

Welker Family, Gratz History, p 450–455.

Pats Family, Pat Scott, pat.scott@comcast.net, awt.ancestry.com.

Elizabeth Messerschmidt, Pennsylvania Church Records - Adams, Berks, and Lancaster Counties, 1729–1881 about Elizabeth Messerschmidt.

Peters Research, Michael McCormick, Enduring Legacy, Gardners, PA, Feb 2009.

Peters household, 1850 United States Federal Census, Union, PA, 288, ancestry.com & Microfilm, PA State Library, Hbg, PA.

Maria Peters, Death notice, Lewisburg Chronicle, Oct. 1852 c/o Union County Historical Society, Maggie Miller, hstorici@ptd.net.

Jacob Wert, Wert family, Onetree, ancestry.com.

Elizabeth Wert death record, Extract from County Death records, 1893–1906.

Shoop family information, Are you my cousin, Harold Ward, haroldw1 @juno.com, awt.ancestry.com.

Shoop family information, Northumberland Co County, PA 1777–1865, Stone Valley Lutheran, www.ancestry.com.

Johannes Schup, Stone Valley Cemetery, Robert Straub, Dalmatia, PA, Section A, Row 16, Grave 30.

Wert Family, Jonathan Wert, www.mdi-wert.com.

Sarah Wertz, David C Paul, Owner: dcpnascar7781, ancestry.com.

The Lunnys, William Lunny, rlunny@msn.com, awt.ancestry.com.

Frank Rowe, FHL, Pedigree chart, www.familysearch.org.

William Rowe, Family Data Collection, Individual Records, www.ancestry.com, Edmund West, comp.

William Rowe, Rowe family, Onetree, ancestry.com.

William Rowe, Descendants of Frank (Rau) Rowe, Evelyn S. Hartman.

Johann Wilhelm Frantz, Descendants of Johann Wilhelm Frantz, Evelyn S. Hartman.

Adam Frantz, Frantz family, Onetree, ancestry.com.

Gieseman family information, Mary Smith.

Franz-Gieseman marriage record, October 1811, source unknown.

Susanna Franz, St. John's Congr., 17 feb 1826, Mifflin, Dauphin Co, PA, Gert, gert@foothill.net.

Franz-Gieseman marriage record, October 1811, Lykens Valley lower church (David's Reformed) Millersburg, Upper Paxton, Dauphin Co, 1774–1844.

Susanna Franz, St. John's Congr.17 feb 1826, Mifflin, Dauphin Co, PA, Gert Mysliwski, gert@foothill.net.

Michael Lyman, David R. Layman, Biography, source unknown.

Lehman-Klein marriage record, June 28, 1818, Church Book records 4.

Lehman-Klein marriage record, Marriages at Trinity Lutheran Church, Lancaster Co, PA, Joan E. Kahler, Charles.Kahler@worldnet.att.net.

David R. Layman, Biography, source unknown.

John Rieman, 1850 United States Federal Census, Year: 1850; Census Place: York South Ward, York, Pennsylvania; Roll: M432_839; Page: 74B; Image: 722.

Michael Oberland, 1798, #3, York County Births 1730–1900, Humphrey, Gert Mysliwski, gert@foothill.net.

Michael Oberland, St. Matthews Lutheran Church records, Hanover, PA, Helda Kline.

Warner family information, JWerner.txt, Don Varner, DRVarner@aol.com.

Maria Catharina Werner, baptismal record, St Jacobs Lutheran Church, Vicki Kessler, Secretary, saintjacobslutheranchurch@msn.com.

Gipe Family of Chanceford Twp., York Co, 1997, Harry A. Diehl, p 1–5.266 William Anderson, FHL, Pedigree chart, www.familysearch.com.

William Anderson, February, 1840, Abstracts of Wills, Chapman, PA.

Anderson family information, Bob Anderson, PA, rmorris@ptd.net.

Anderson family information, Lisa betts, betts@sprintmail.com.

Catharina Arnold, Reformed Church Records in Eastern Pennsylvania, Copied by Dr. William J. Hinke, Church Records of Zion's or Stone Valley Lutheran and Reformed Church, http://www.mahantongo.org.

Arnold family, FHL, Pedigree Chart, Ancestral File, www.familysearch.org.

Bordner family information, Roger Cramer, rogercubs@aol.com.

Descendants of Philip Jacob Bortner, John Getz, jgetz@iu.net.

Children of Johann Michael Emerich, The Bordner & Burtner Families, H.W. Bordner, Washington DC, 1967, p 10.

Emerick family information, Ancestors & Descendants of Johann Michael Emerich of New York 1709–1979, O. S. Emrich, Ann Fenley, Dayton, OH.

Gaugler family information, author unknown.

Gaugler Notes, Dauphin County Courthouse, Ronald W. Huber, Salfordsville, PA, 1978.

Mary Gaugler, Mount Zion United Brethren Church Cemetery, Snyder Co, PA, Shaffer & Arnold, 1904, www.rootsweb.com.

Wriah Kelly, Pennsylvania, Death Certificates, 1906–1963 [database on-line]. Provo, UT, USA: Ancestry.com Operations, Inc., 2014.

Wm Kelly, Mount Zion United Brethren Church Cemetery, Snyder Co, PA, Shaffer & Arnold, 1904, www.rootsweb.com.

Shaffer family information, Debra Kassing, dk2_inc@msn.com.

Elizabeth Kelly, Mount Zion United Brethren Church Cemetery, Snyder Co, PA, Shaffer & Arnold, 1904, www.rootsweb.com.

Keefer, Kiefer file, Northumberland Co County Historical Society, Sunbury, PA.

My Family, Dillon, Kelly, Peterson, etc., Clint Dillon, treegnome@msn.com, awt.ancestry.com.

Lycoming County PA & Related Families, Harold E. Bower, Jr., harold.bower @usa.com, awt.ancestry.com.

Keefer Book, Pedigree Chart, The Family of Frederick Kieffer, Chapter V, p 1318, E.G. Keefer, 1997.

David Kieffer, Union Cemetery Co, Delongs Reformed Church records, Bowers, PA.

Peter Kieffer Sr, NSSAR Ecord copy, SAR application, Samuel L Savidge, Northumberland, PA, Nat # 114561, State #8464, Jun 1978.

Daniel Keefer, Probate files, 1862, Northumberland County Courthouse, Reg of Wills, Sunbury, Bk 6, p170, PA, Robyn Jackson, genealogylover@msn.com, 2008.

John Conrad Bucher, Bucher family, Onetree, ancestry.com.

Livezly-Culen marriage record, Gloria Dei Church, 916 S Swanson, Philadelphia, PA 19147, bk 18, p 6.

History of Pennsylvania volunteers, 1861–5; prepared in compliance with acts of the legislature, by Samuel P. Bates. Collection: Making of America Books History of Pennsylvania volunteers, 1861–5; prepared in compliance with acts of the legislature, by Samuel P. Bates, 1827–1902.

http://155thpa.tripod.com/id2.html - see pictures of the uniforms here.

http://civilwar.gratzpa.org/2011/01/tower-city-porter-township-centennial-civil-war-veterans-list/

http://civilwar.gratzpa.org/2012/01/alexander-f-thompson-senator-and-attorney/

http://civilwar.gratzpa.org/2012/01/alexander-f-thompson-senator-and-attorney/;

http://www.findagrave.com/cgi-bin/fg.cgi?page=gr&GRid=117381891

http://civilwar.gratzpa.org/2012/01/alexander-f-thompson-senator-and-attorney/

http://civilwar.gratzpa.org/2012/04/2012-additions-to-civil-war-veterans-list-g-to-i/

http://civilwar.gratzpa.org/veterans/Charles McKean, "Edinburgh: 3. 1750 Onwards" in: The Oxford Companion to Scottish History, Edited by Michael Lynch, OUP, 2007

http://coalregionhistorychronicles.blogspot.com/2008/09/explosion-at-york-farm-colliery.html

http://en.wikipedia.org/wiki/Ludlow_Massacre

http://explorepahistory.com/story.php?storyId=1-9-4

http://files.usgwarchives.net/pa/schuylkill/history/local/munsell/hist0012.txt

http://files.usgwarchives.net/pa/schuylkill/military/civilwar/captured.txt

http://historynewsnetwork.org/article/623

http://quod.lib.umich.edu/m/moa/aby3439.0004.001/818?page=root;sid=41cea510eb7635c5b3e50413737b17fb;size=100;view=image;q1=One+Hundred+And+Fifty-Fifth+Regiment

http://quod.lib.umich.edu/m/moa/aby3439.0004.001/818?page=root;sid=41cea510eb7635c5b3e50413737b17fb; size=100;view=image;q1=One+Hundred+And+Fifty-Fifth+Regiment History of Pennsylvania volunteers, 1861–5; prepared in compliance with acts of the legislature, by Samuel P. Bates. Collection: Making of America Books

http://quod.lib.umich.edu/m/moa/aby3439.0004.001/818?page=root;sid=41c ea510eb7635c5b3e50413737b17fb;size=100;view=image;q1=One+Hundred+And +Fifty-Fifth+Regiment.

http://ultimatehistoryproject.com/before-the-whiteout-wedding-dresses-and-grooms-outfits.html

http://usminedisasters.com/Mine_Disasters/search_Coal_state.asp?ACC_STATE_NAME=Penn
sylvania&x=11&y=15

http://www.civilwar.org/education/history/warfare-and-logistics/warfare/ richmond.html

http://www.civilwararchive.com/Unreghst/unpacav1.htm#9th

http://www.dailykos.com/story/2013/09/22/1211516/-Sweet-Home-Schuylkill-County-The-PA-
Anthracite-coal-region-1790–1917#

http://www.dailykos.com/story/2013/09/23/1211516/-Sweet-Home-Schuylkill-County-The-PA-
Anthracite-coal-region-1790–1917.

http://www.digitalarchives.state.pa.us/archive.asp?view=ArchiveItems&ArchiveID=17&FL=G
&FID=1194432&LID=1194481

http://www.ebooksread.com/authors-eng/jm-runk—company/commemorative-biographical-
encyclopedia-of-dauphin-county-pennsylvania—contai-urm/page-198-commemorative-biogra-
phical-encyclopedia-of-dauphin-county-pennsylvania—contai-urm.shtml

http://www.findagrave.com/cgi-bin/fg.cgi?page=gr&GRid=62785330

http://www.lancasteratwar.com/2011/12/here-comes-cavalry-part-ii-lochiel .html

http://www.measuringworth.com/uscompare

http://www.measuringworth.com/uscompare/relativevalue.php

http://www.pacivilwar.com/regiment/155th.html

http://www.pacivilwar.com/regiment/191st.html

http://www.pagenweb.org/~schuylkill/castle/castle19.jpg

http://www.rootsweb.ancestry.com/~padauph2/lykinsnews.html

http://zouavedatabase.weebly.com/civil-war-zouave-unit-master-list.html

https://archive.org/stream/troopsundercomma01harr/troopsundercomma01harr_djvu.txt

https://books.google.com/books?id=eCk_AQAAMAAJ&pg=PA159&lpg=PA 159&dq=Bast+%26
+Thompson+Schuylkill+county+mines&source=bl&ots=CW Tape7T1m&sig=Qm3SW59QO91r
eKpIleicM0cI0UU&hl=en&sa=X&ei=9Jj-VPrtCMu0ggTCrYHgDA&ved=0CC4Q6AEwAw#v
=onepage&q=Bast%20%26 %Thompson%20Schuylkill%20county%20mines&f=false

https://books.google.com/books?id=j3NWAAAAYAAJ&pg=PA1080&lpg=PA1080&dq=solomon
+updegrove+d.+1864+georgia&source=bl&ots=8iZFQh28Zi& sig=XR_F0FkDZ9F8_9Bp206AZkt
xp2I&hl=en&sa=X&ved=0CB8Q6AEwAG   oVChMIhbGV5_G7xwIVDOCACh138gBg#v=one
page&q=solomon%20updegrove%20d.%201864%20georgia&f=false; http://www.findagrave.com/
cgi-bin/ fg.cgi?page=gr&GRid=84377395

https://books.google.com/books?id=MTTAAAAIAAJ&pg=PA179&dq=%22daniel+updegrove
%22&hl=en&sa=X&ved=0CC4Q6AEwA2oVChMI_67k2M KnxwIVy6CACh1IaQDu#v=onepage
&q=daniel%20updegrove&f=false, Weekly Notes of Cases Argued and Determined in the
Supreme Court ..., Volume 20

https://books.google.com/books?id=rRwQAAAAYAAJ&pg=PA308&lpg=PA308&dq=Captain+John+McMillan%E2%80%99s+company,+Colonel+Fenton%E2%80%99s+regiment,+of+the+Pennsylvania+Militia&source=bl&ots=YpSCK5C7sj&sig=hKIwaYSwScmid-HNUo_kavB2_EE&hl=en&sa=X&ei=_cpfVfnLMczBsAXt-YAI&ved=0CDIQ6AEwBA#v=onepage&q=Captain %20John %20McMillan%E2%80%99s%20company%2C%20Colonel%20Fenton%E2%80%99s%20regiment%2C%20of%20the%20Pennsylvania%20Militia&f=false

https://books.google.com/books?id=xr-rrOqOPysC&pg=PA553&lpg=PA553&dq=Lochiel+-Cavalry+and+libby+prison&source=bl&ots=31SzP5eI6A&sig=g46Cqj-M4kAZOwYpx5fCh84j6Oo&hl=en&sa=X&ved=0CEMQ6AEwBmoVChMIgr6vufqnxwIVw4MNCh0nyA2A#v=onepage&q=Lochiel%20&f=false A Scout to East Tennessee by the Lochiel Cavalry. Anecdotes, Poetry, and Incidents of the War: North and South: 1860–1865, By Frank Moore

https://books.google.com/books?id=zagAAAAYAAJ&printsec=frontcover&source=gbs_ge_summary_r&cad=0#v=onepage&q=hensel&f=false; After the Reserves: An Unofficial History of the 190th and 191st Pennsylvania Volunteer Infantry Regiments, June 1, 1864 through June 28, 1865

http://www.pareserves.com/files/pdf_files/AFTER%20THE%20RESERVES.PDF   Under the Maltese Cross (1910)

https://en.wikipedia.org/wiki/Libby_Prison_Escape

https://www.lycoming.edu/umarch/chronicles/2011/2Evangelical.pdf

Luther Reily Kelker, History of Dauphin County, Pennsylvania: With Genealogical Memoirs, Volumes 1–2, p. 1080

Schuylkill County Firefighting by Michael R. Glore and Michael J. Kitsock. Arcadia Publishing, 2010.

The West Schuylkill Herald, Jan 3, 1901, Jeffrey A. Brown, ntrprz@dmv.com

Collection: Making of America Books Tower City, Porter Township Centennial book, 1868–1968, Records of Jim Thompson, jbthompson @compuserve.com

http://archive.org/stream/lykenswilliamsva00barr/lykenswilliamsva00barr_djvu.txt

http://archive.org/stream/lykenswilliamsva00barr/lykenswilliamsva00barr_djvu.txt   Harrisburg Patriot Sept. 7, 1891

http://archive.org/stream/lykenswilliamsva00barr/lykenswilliamsva00barr_djvu.txt   Lykens-Williams Valley directory and pictorial review Map population density of the United States from the 1810 census www.wfu.edu Lykens-Williams Valley directory and pictorial review Annals of Buffalo Valley, Pennsylvania, 1755–1855, Linn, John Blair

http://explorepahistory.com/story.php?storyId=1-9-E&chapter=1 (Dauphin from state data)

http://www.carnegielibrary.org/research/ Lykens-Williams Valley history - directory and pictorial review

http://www.wtwp.org/ Harrisburg Patriot, January 18, 1906 Harrisburg Patriot

http://www.dcnr.state.pa.us/cs/groups/public/documents/document/dcnr_009325.pdf

http://www.dcnr.state.pa.us/cs/groups/public/documents/document/dcnr_009325.pdf

http://www.dol.gov/dol/aboutdol/history/coalstrike.htm

http://www.familysearch.org Harrisburg Patriot, August 23, 1917 Lykens - Williams Valley History Directory J. Allen Barrett ancestry.com

http://www.msha.gov/District/Dist_01/History/history.htm

http://www.pbs.org/wned/war-of-1812/timeline/ Lykens-Williams Valley history,

http://www.portal.state.pa.us/portal/server.pt/community/events/4279/

http://www.reviewhttp://archive.org/stream/lykenswilliamsva00barr/lykenswilliamsva00barr _djvu.txt

http://www.unioncountyhistoricalsociety.orgAnnals of Buffalo Valley, Pennsylvania, 1755–1855 Linn, John Blair 1850 United States Census Annals of Buffalo Valley, Pennsylvania, 1755–1855 Linn, John Blair Lykens-Williams Valley history - directory and pictorial

Brief history of York County PA by George R. Powell; pg 28; copyright 1906

Catherine Duncan, Death certificate, Northumberland Co County Register of Wills, Sunbury, PA

Charley Duncan, Baptisms of Infants, Zion Evan Luth Register, 1851–1892, Sunbury, PA, p101

Charlotte Layman, Duncan family information, Stephanie Gormley

County of Northumberland Pennsylvania www.northumberlandco.org

David McCloud, Probate files, 1864, Northumberland County Courthouse, Reg of Wills, Sunbury, Bk 5, p261, PA

David R. Layman, Biography, source unknown

Donkert household, 1880 United States Census, Northumberland Co, PA, ancestry.com & Microfilm, PA State Library, Hbg, PA

Duncan death certificate, #0030852, #90924, Northumberland Co, PA, Department of Vital records, New Castle, PA

Duncan family information, 1870 United States Census, York Co, PA, Roll M5931468, p 545, Image 700, ancestry.com & Microfilm, PA State Library, Hbg, PA

Duncan family information, Jack Lehman, North Charleston, SC

Duncan family information, Stephanie Gormley, PA, 1989

Duncan household, 1900 United States Census, microfilm image, PA State Library. Died Sunbury, PA,

Duncan household, 1900 United States Census, microfilm image, PA State Library

Duncan household, 1910 United States Census, Northumberland Co, PA, ED 0118, Visit 0155, ancestry.com & Microfilm, PA State Library, Hbg, PA

Duncan-Layman marriage record, #8855, Northumberland Co, PA, 1899, Northumberland Co County Register of Wills, Sunbury, PA

Duncan-Layman marriage record, April 20, 1899, Edward C. Eisley

Dungan household, 1870 United States Census, Northumberland Co, PA, ancestry.com & Microfilm, PA State Library, Hbg, PA

Dungard household, 1870 United States Census, Northumberland Co, PA, ancestry.com & Microfilm, PA State Library, Hbg, PA

ED 134, Image 0913, ancestry.com & Microfilm, PA State Library, Hbg, PA

Elmira Layman, Bethel ME Cemetery, p 151, Jerome K. Hively, Brogue, PA

en.wikipedia.org/wiki/Airville%2C_Pennsylvania

files.usgwarchives.net/pa/northumberland/areahistory/bell0011.txt 153 Bell's History of Northumberland County Pennsylvania transcribed by Tony Rebuck for use in USGenWeb Archives pages 309 – 311 & 705 – 707 378 http://en.wikipedia.org"Vikings" and "Scottish trades in early modern era" http://www.portal.state.pa.us/ Pennsylvania history – Independence to Civil War

First Electric Light Historical Marker, www.explorepahistory.com/hmarker .php?markerId=1-A-399

Hannah Artilla Duncan, Baptisms of Infants, Zion Evan Luth Register, 1851–1892, Sunbury, PA, p94

Hawkins household, 1900 United States Census, Northumberland Co, PA, ancestry.com & Microfilm, PA State Library, Hbg, PA.

Hawkins household, 1920 United States Census, Cook, IL, ancestry.com & Microfilm, PA State Library, Hbg, PA

History of Pennsylvania agriculture http://www.portal.state.pa.us

How the Homestead Act Transformed America, www.smithsonianmag.com/ history-archaeology/How-the-Homestead-Act-Transformed-America.html

http://books.google.com/books?id=X6fhAAAAMAAJ&pg=PA542&lpg=PA542&dq=W.+C.+Calhoun+1901+copper+mine+swindler&source=bl&ots=V-k0i6Js Dx&sig=3BQzIxEdNPol7Cai ZS2G3kDiW6g&hl=en&sa=X&ei=ZceEUrLQOqn hiAKNmIHYCg&ved=0CCwQ6AEwA Q#v= onepage&q=W.%20C.%2cCalhoun %201901%20copper%20mine%20swindler&f=false, The Copper Handbook, Volumes 8, By Horace Jared Stevens, Walter Harvey Weed,

http://en.wikipedia.org/ History of Elizabethtown PA

http://en.wikipedia.org/Flatboats http://www.distancebetweencities.net/

http://www.houseofnames.com

http://en.wikipedia.org/William McKinley 200 http://www.yorkblog.com/ York Furnace Bridge

http://files.usgwarchives.net/pa/york/history/gibson/chanceford-twp.txt The Township of Chanceford, York County, PA, B. F. Porter, M. D., 1886 -

http://liveauctions.holabirdamericana.com/CO-Copperfield-Fremont-County-1900-Colorado-Copper-Mining-Company-Stock-Certificate-Fenske-C_ i10680523 Colorado Copper Mining Co.

http://sharing.ancestry.com/3045477?h=16e789

http://www.measuringworth.com/ppowerus/, Measuringworth.com

http://www.cityofsunbury.com/Blacksmithing History 1 - http://www.appal tree.net/aba/hist1.htm

http://www.cyberdriveillinois.com/GenealogyMWeb/ODPHdeathsearch

http://www.cyberdriveillinois.com/GenealogyMWeb/ODPHdeathsearch.1916-

http://www.donicht.de/lutheraner.htm Old Lutheran immigration fever,

http://www.gdhspa.org/Dover/flood%20of%201884.htm The Inundation of York, Penna: A Graphic Description of the Great Flood: with an Account of the Violent Rain Storm of June 25, 1884 (Google eBook) - F. L. Spangler, York Daily Printing House, 1884 Flood of 1884

http://www.gendisasters.com/data1/ny/earthquakes/eastcoast-earthquake-aug1884.htm 1884 August Earthquake 399 http://www.genealogy.com/ 24_land.html Revolutionary War Bounty Land Grants

http://www.mahantongo.org/mmhps/stoneval.htm a link from the Northumberland Historical Society found on the City of Sunbury website

http://www.mahantongo.org/mmhps/stoneval.htm Zion Stone Valley Church

http://www.mayoclinic.com Symptoms of nephritis

http://www.healthline.com, Symptoms of cystitis

http://www.phmc.state.pa.us Pennsylvania Historical Museum Commission

http://www.phmc.state.pa.us/ - Lancaster County http://www.padutchcountry.com Marietta, Lancaster Co. PA

http://www.portal.state.pa.us Pennsylvania Historical & Museum Commission

http://www.portal.state.pa.us/portal/server.pt/community/overview_of_pennsylvania_history/4281 Pennsylvania Historic & Museum Commission -

http://www.portal.state.pa.us/portal/server.pt/community/pennsylvania%27s_agricultural_history/2584 Pennsylvania Historic & Museum Commission,

http://www.wlsessays.net/files/WesterhausEmigrations.pdf The Confessional Lutheran Emigrations from Prussia and Saxony Around 1839,

http://www.yorkblog.com/How did they get across the wide Susquehanna when there were no bridges?

http://yorkcountypa.gov/History York County PA http://web.archive.org/ — Agriculture in Lancaster PA

Jefferson Copper Mining Co. Colorado - Scripopholy.com

http://scripophily.net/jecomicoco19.html

John Reiman, York Co, PA Will index, Gert Mysliwski, gert@foothill.net. http://en.wikipedia.org/ —Lancaster County

Joseph P Leyman, Evergreen Cemetery, Index files and lot lists, #5435, Lot SG 157, Maple Gr Pt 6, vault 5/9/box, permit #4976, Chicago, IL

Joseph Pierce Layman, death record, Illinois Statewide Death Index, 1916-

Joseph Pierce Layman, State of IL, Dept of Public Health, DVS, Reg #4976, Primary Dt #3104, Cook, IL, Feb 1924.

Klein household, 1820 United States Census, Lancaster Co, PA, ancestry.com & Microfilm, PA State Library, Hbg, PA

Layman household, 1800 United States Census, Centre Co, PA, ancestry.com & Microfilm, PA State Library, Hbg, PA

Layman/Lehman family information, Files, NCHS, The Hunter House, Sunbury, PA

Laymen household, 1910 United States Census, Northumberland Co, PA, ED 0114, Visit 0085, ancestry.com & Microfilm, PA State Library, Hbg, PA

Laynon household, 1900 United States Census, Northumberland Co, PA, ancestry.com & Microfilm, PA State Library, Hbg, PA

Lehman-Klein marriage record, June 28, 1818, Church Book records 4

Lehman-Klein marriage record, Marriages at Trinity Lutheran Church, Lancaster Co, PA, Joan E. Kahler, Charles.Kahler@worldnet.att.net.

Lehman-Oberlander marriage, source unknown

Leyman family information, source unknown

Lottie Duncan, Pomfret Manor Cemetery, Sam Derr, Sunbury, PA, lot 130-B

Lottie V Willard death certificate, File #29987, Reg #19, #3505042, February 1936, Department of Vital Records, New Castle, PA

Lottie V. Willard, Lottie Duncan, Pomfret Manor Cemetery, Sam Derr, Sunbury, PA, lot 130-B

Lyman household, 1850 United States Census, York Co, PA, Roll M432-

Lyman household, 1860 United States Census, York Co, PA, ancestry.com & Microfilm, PA State Library, Hbg, PA

Lyman household, 1870 United States Census, York Co, PA, Roll M593 1468, p 545, Image 700, ancestry.com & Microfilm, PA, State Library, Hbg, PA

Lyman household, 1880 United States Census, York Co, PA, FHL 1255208, Film T9-1208, p 640D, www.familysearch.org

McCloud household, 1860 United States Census, Northumberland Co, PA, Series M653, Roll 1149, p 71, ancestry.com & Microfilm, PA State Library, Hbg, PA

McCloud household, 1870 United States Census, Northumberland Co, PA, ancestry.com & Microfilm, PA State Library, Hbg, PA

McCloud household, 1880 United States Census, Northumberland Co, PA, ancestry.com & Microfilm, PA State Library, Hbg, PA

McCloud-Frye, Marriage, Northumberland County, SS, #2856, Register & Recorder, Sunbury, PA, Oct 1890, Market St, Sunbury, PA.

McLeod household, 1850 United States Census, Northumberland Co, PA, ancestry.com & Microfilm, PA State Library, Hbg, PA

Melinda Duncan, Cemetery record, Apr 1933, A genealogists Guide to Burials in Northumberland Co, PA, Vol I, Meiser & Meiser, 1989

Michael Layman, Bethel ME Cemetery, p 151, Jerome K. Hively, Brogue, PA

National Heart and Lung Institute, What Causes Pneumonia? www.nhlbi .nih.gov

Layman Family information from Marc Thompson

Northumberland Co County Register of Wills

Oberlander household, 1830 United States Census, York Co, PA, ancestry.com & Microfilm, PA State Library, Hbg, PA

Oberlander household, 1840 United States Census, York Co, PA, ancestry.com & Microfilm, PA State Library, Hbg, PA

Oberlander household, 1850 United States Census, York Co, PA, Roll M432 839, p 839, ancestry.com & Microfilm, PA State Library, Hbg, PA

Oberlander household, 1860 United States Census, York Co, PA, ancestry.com & Microfilm, PA State Library, Hbg, PA

Oberlander household, 1870 United States Census, York Co, PA, ancestry.com & Microfilm, PA State Library, Hbg, PA

Oberlander household, 1880 United States Census, York Co, PA, FHL 1255207, Film T9-1207, p 599C, www.familysearch.org

Sarah Oberlander, Overlander-Kipe marriage record, #662-59, Calendar of Vital Records of the Counties of York & Adams

Pennsylvania in the Civil War www.wikipedia.org Brief history of York County PA by George R. Powell; pg 28; copyright 1906

Pennsylvania, 1851–92, Zion Evangelical Church, www.ancestry.com William Duncan, Baptisms of Infants, Zion Evan Luth Register, 1851–1892, Sunbury, PA, p41

Probate files, 1874, Rep 42, Bk 342, York County Archives, York, PA, Deborah Hershey, Elizabethtown, PA, Dec 2008

Rebecca Layman, Pomfret Manor Cemetery, Sam Derr, Sunbury, PA, lot 130-B

Rebecca Lehman (Layman) death certificate, #105066, Reg # 456, #3457529, November 1921, Department of Vital Records, New Castle, PA

Rieman household, 1820 United States Census, York Co, PA, ancestry.com & Microfilm, PA State Library, Hbg, PA

Robyn Jackson, genealogylover@msn.com, 2008

Sallie Duncan, Cemetery record, Apr 1933, A genealogists Guide to Burials in Northumberland Co, PA, Vol I, Meiser & Meiser, 1989

Sarah Duncan, Baptisms of Infants, Zion Evan Luth Register, 1851–1892, Sunbury, PA, p41

Sarah Oberlander, Probate files, 1874, Rep 42, York County Archives, York, PA, Deborah Hershey, Elizabethtown, PA, Dec 2008.

wiki.answers.com/Q/Why_did_people_leave_Germany_for_America_in_the_late_1800's?

Willard household, 1920 United States Census, Northumberland Co, PA, Roll T625 1611, p 7A, ED 134, Image 0913, ancestry.com & Microfilm, PA State Library, Hbg, PA

Willard household, 1930 United States Census, Northumberland Co, PA, Roll T626 2091, p 7A, ED 71, Image 0681, ancestry.com & Microfilm, PA State Library, Hbg, PA

William Duncan, Baptisms of Infants, Zion Evan Luth Register, 1851–1892, Sunbury, PA, p41

William Duncan, Northumberland Co County, Pennsylvania, 1851–92, Zion Evangelical Church, www.ancestry.com

William Duncan, Pomfret Manor Cemetery, Sam Derr, Sunbury, PA, lot 130-B

William Duncan, Pomfret Manor Cemetery, Sunbury, Northumberland Co, PA, NCHS, The Hunter House, Sunbury, PA

William Duncan, Probate files, July 1906, Northumberland County Courthouse, Reg of Wills, Bk 12, p424, Sunbury, PA, Robyn Jackson, genealogylover@msn.com, 2008

William Duncan, Probate files, July 1906, Northumberland County Courthouse, Reg of Wills, Bk 12, p424, Sunbury, PA, Robyn Jackson, genealogylover@msn.com, 2008.

Duncan family information, Jack Lehman, North Charleston, SC

Wm Duncan death certificate, #0030852, #90924, Northumberland Co, PA, Department of Vital records, New Castle, PA

Wm Duncan, Northumberland Co County Courthouse, Register of Wills, 11-27-1901

http://cigarhistory.info/Cigar_History/History_1878–1915.html

http://en.wikipedia.org/wiki/Dyeing

http://en.wikipedia.org/wiki/History_of_cancer

http://en.wikipedia.org/wiki/Pennsylvania

http://en.wikipedia.org/wiki/Pennsylvania_Canal

http://en.wikipedia.org/wiki/Samuel_Gompers

http://en.wikipedia.org/wiki/Snyder_County,_Pennsylvania

http://explorepahistory.com/story.php?storyId=1-9-10

http://explorepahistory.com/story.php?storyId=1-9-21

http://www.allentownsd.org/Page/16

http://www.ancestry.com/name-origin?surname=bordner

http://www.ancestry.com/name-origin?surname=gaugler

http://www.phme.state.pa.us/bhp/AQL/context/Central_Limestone_Valleys.pdf

http://en.wikipedia.org/wiki/Pennsylvania_Lumber_Museum

http://www.princeton.edu/history/people/display_person.xml?netid=hartog&interview=yes

http://www.prrths.com

http://www.shmoop.com/1920s/economy.html

http://www.wiley.com/legacy/products/subject/business/forbes/ford.html

http://en.wikipedia.org/wiki/Rural_electrification#United_States

http://zerbetownship.org/history.asp

http://en.wikipedia.org/wiki/Ashland,_Pennsylvania

http://en.wikipedia.org/wiki/Brakeman

http://en.wikipedia.org/wiki/Federal_Employers_Liability_Act

http://www.pinegrovetownship.com/History.html

http://www.questia.com/library/history/social-history/women-in-19th-century-america

http://www.answers.com/topic/sewing-machine

http://www.answers.com/topic/clothing-industry

http://www.nps.gov/civilwar/search-regiments-detail.htm?regiment_id=UPA0172RIX 32

http://en.wikipedia.org/wiki/Pennsylvania_in_the_American_Civil_War

http://www.etymonline.com/cw/draft.htm

http://en.wikipedia.org/wiki/Militia_%28United_States%29#Civil_War

http://en.wikipedia.org/wiki/Peninsula_Campaign

http://en.wikipedia.org/wiki/History_of_education_in_the_United_States#One-room_school houses

http://en.wikipedia.org/wiki/Port_Trevorton,_Pennsylvania

http://www.portal.state.pa.us/portal/server.pt/community/pennsylvania%27s_agricultural_history/2584

http://www.portal.state.pa.us/portal/server.pt/community/pennsylvania%27s_agricultural_history/2584/

North_and_West_Branch.pdf

http://relationships.blurtit.com/1647575/what-was-the-average-family-size-in-the-19th-century

http://en.wikipedia.org/wiki/Pennsylvania_in_the_American_Civil_War

http://en.wikipedia.org/wiki/Shamokin_%28village%29

http://en.wikipedia.org/wiki/Sunbury,_Pennsylvania

http://en.wikipedia.org/wiki/Pennsylvania_Canal

http://en.wikipedia.org/wiki/File:Pennsylvania_canals.png

http://en.wikipedia.org/wiki/Main_Line_of_Public_Works

http://en.wikipedia.org/wiki/Pennsylvania_Railroad

http://explorepahistory.com/story.php?storyId=1-9-10

http://hatbox.com/hat-history.cfm 50 http://en.wikipedia.org/wiki/Mad_hatter_disease

http://en.wikipedia.org/wiki/History_of_the_Ursulines_in_New_Orleans

http://en.wikipedia.org/wiki/Ashland,_Pennsylvania

http://www.rootsweb.ancestry.com/~wibrown/naming.htm

http://www.ereferencedesk.com/resources/state-history-timeline/pennsylvania .html

http://www.timelines.ws/states/PENNSYLVANIA.HTML

http://www.datesandevents.org/american-timelines/38-pennsylvania-history-timeline.htm

https://en.wikipedia.org/wiki/Timeline_of_Harrisburg,_Pennsylvania_history

https://en.wikipedia.org/wiki/List_of_Pennsylvania_hurricanes

http://www.hunimex.com/warwick/diseases.html

http://www.behindthename.com

Index

www.ingramcontent.com/pod-product-compliance
Lightning Source LLC
Chambersburg PA
CBHW081400270326
41930CB00015B/3363